D1489739

Critical Connection
A Practical Guide to
Parenting Young
Teens

ANDY KERCKHOFF

Andy Kerckhoff is a middle school teacher and the author of the blog *Growing Up Well*. He and his wife have been married for twenty years and have two teenage children.

Kerckhoff has served in various educational roles for over twenty years, including as an elementary school principal in Whitefish, Montana, and a high school teacher in Dallas, Texas. He currently serves as a seventh-grade English and World Geography teacher at Westminster Christian Academy in Saint Louis, Missouri.

White Orchard Press
Critical Connection: A Practical Guide for Parenting Young Teens
Andy Kerckhoff

Copy Editor: Meghan Pinson
Cover Design: Andrew Kristyan

Published in the United States by White Orchard Press
ISBN 978-0-9911318-0-8

Version 1.0
Printed by CreateSpace, a DBA of On-Demand Publishing, LLC

"A child is a person who is going to carry on what you have started. He is going to sit where you are sitting, and when you are gone, attend to those things which you think are important. You may adopt all the policies you please, but how they are carried out depends on him. He will assume control of your cities, your states, and your nation. He is going to move in and take your churches, your schools, your universities, and your corporations. All your books are going to be judged, praised, or condemned by him. The fate of humanity is in his hands."

Abraham Lincoln

"When I was a boy of fourteen, my father was so ignorant I could hardly stand to have the old man around. But when I got to be twenty-one, I was astonished at how much the old man had learned in seven years."

Mark Twain

What People Are Saying About Critical Connection

"Parenting in the 21st century is incredibly challenging. The messages we receive about how to raise successful, well-adjusted, happy teenagers are myriad and contradictory, and our attempts at appropriate boundaries and guidelines for our kids are often fraught with doubt, conflict, and surrender. In *Critical Connection: A Practical Guide for Parenting Young Teens*, Andy Kerckhoff provides invaluable insights from his practitioner's experience as a husband, son, father, and teacher of teens. Any parent would benefit from reading this book and seriously grappling with its truths, insights, and suggestions, especially in the area of social media and its profound impact on today's teens. It is not a "do list" for perfect parenting; it is a penetrating, personal perspective on effective parenting in a complex, technological, and rapidly changing world."

Jim Marsh
Westminster Christian Academy, Head of School Emeritus
Director of the Van Lunen Center, a Center of Calvin College
Parent and Grandparent

"I am excited for those who have the opportunity to read *Critical Connection*. I appreciate Kerckhoff's honesty, as well as the hope and optimism he brings to this difficult yet rewarding time in parenting. He describes the toils yet captures the joys that come with raising young teens. This book navigates parents in understanding the heart of their child. In that navigating, parents come to understand their own hearts and how their own story affects their children.

Too many parenting books prescribe the quick fix or the "5 Easy Steps to Parenting," but Kerckhoff provides a refreshingly honest approach. His book offers freedom for parents to truly connect to their own hearts as well as to the heart of their children. As a Licensed Professional Counselor and seminary professor, I recommend this book for all parents who are seeking encouragement, hope, and insight."

Mark Pfuetze, MDiv, LPC
Covenant Theological Seminary

"Adolescents don't come with a manual, but this book is close. *Critical Connection* is coming from a parent, coach, and teacher who engages adolescents daily. The practical information and thought-provoking statements will challenge you to think of parenting in a broader light. Whether you feel ill-equipped as a parent or very equipped, this book will draw you to a deeper understanding of parenting beyond."

Craig Walseth
Middle School Guidance Counselor

"For any parent who has taken the journey through the middle school years knows, it can be a little like navigating a minefield blindfolded. It's tough to know what to expect. *Critical Connections* will help parents to form up the right framework to build a solid foundation, not only for high school, but also for the college years and life beyond.

A strong, authentic emotional bond between a parent and child is the single most important aspect of raising children today, and this book supplies just the right ingredients that will help you discover how your child is made and what to do with them when they hit middle school. From the top twenty tips that will help your child succeed in school all the way to helping them understand a career path, *Critical Connection* will give you the hands-on wisdom and will provide success in establishing a stronger heart-to-heart connection.

Andy Kerckhoff's book is a must-have tool that every mom and dad should get to help them navigate those tumultuous years. It's the best resource tool I have read in three decades!"

Ward Wiebe
Director of K-West, a summer camp for boys and girls (12-14)

CONTENTS

ACKNOWLEDGMENTS

I would like to thank my wife for supporting me in this endeavor and for being my primary inspiration for parenting and teaching. Without her, I would cut a lot of corners and be far less of a man. I want to thank my son for being a truly awesome kid who makes me proud every day. I am a lucky man to have a son who makes me so proud and is such a good friend. I want to thank my daughter for having so much patience, strength, and joy every day, in spite of her many challenges. She is an inspiration to all who know her.

I wish to thank my copy editor, Meghan Pinson, for her outstanding professional work and personal encouragement in this project. Without her, this book would be pure amateurism. I also wish to thank my friends who have given me valuable feedback and encouragement throughout this project: Rachel Rountree, Laura Smith, Melinda Sims, Scott James, Yancey Arrington, and Mike Weinberg. Without you, I would have never attempted such a big project, and I am so glad I took your advice and kept plugging away at it.

PREFACE

Over the last 25 years of teaching K-12 students, I have seen a disturbing trend. After they leave elementary school, children who are otherwise healthy, intelligent, and well cared for by their parents begin to show signs of neglect. I see it all the time, even though it seems unlikely, considering where I teach: in a private religious middle school in a suburb of St. Louis, Missouri. Despite their privileged upbringing and capable parents, too many kids are left to their own devices between the ages of ten and fourteen.

What these parents don't realize is that when they disengage from their adolescent children, they leave their kids to figure things out for themselves at a time when their wisdom and guidance are desperately needed. I wrote this book in the hope of helping parents teach their children to grow up well. A little more understanding and a few strategic changes can improve the whole family dynamic.

This book will not tell you how to become a perfect parent. Perfect parenting is a dangerous myth, and this book will not help you create a 53-point plan for the perfect family. In fact, a major theme here is avoiding the extreme of being too controlling; helicopter parents can be just as harmful as hands-off parents. My hope is that you will find something interesting, thought-provoking, and helpful in each chapter; maybe not a specific action, but a new understanding and a better attitude toward a specific stage of development. Either way, just one change at the right time can be incredibly helpful in the life of a child. Sometimes the biggest problems are solved with the smallest changes.

Most importantly, I hope that you will be encouraged to listen to, ask questions of, learn from, pray for, and train your child in a more meaningful, honest, and peaceful way. I hope that you will come to understand how critical your relationship with your child is, and that you can make all the difference in helping your child become a healthy, happy, responsible young adult.

Make your plans, but set realistic goals and spread them out over a reasonable timeframe. Pray for wisdom, strength, and patience. These things are never easy, but nothing worthwhile ever is, and raising a child well is the most noble task in the world.

BE THE PARENT

Those who believe that there is one way, or "God's way," to raise children will be disappointed by my book. I don't believe there is a formula for success when it comes to raising healthy and happy children, but there are good practices and bad practices. There are things that generally work and things that generally do not work.

The key to being a good parent is to continually pursue better practices and attitudes. We need to be constantly seeking a better way—by praying for wisdom, talking with other devoted parents, reading books, observing happy families, and trying to get better at helping our kids grow up well. We need to become better lovers and leaders of our kids.

The real dangers are parents who do not examine their ways. The parents who simply react, blindly following their own parents' ways, like the father who shuts down when he feels awkward or encounters conflict, a coping mechanism he picked up from his father. The father may not realize that he is giving the cold shoulder to his child, but it is a clamp on the parent-child relationship.

On the other hand, many parents' default mode is to do the opposite of what their parents would have done. I know a young mom whose parents used to vent every little frustration by pacing, yelling, ranting and raving; now she can't yell at her own kids. She is too calm too often, and her kids get away with murder.

These are examples of knee-jerk parenting. These moms and dads don't think first, then act. Instead, they react first, then regret later. They do what feels right in the moment instead of seeking wisdom beforehand. They do not consult wise friends, grandparents, experts, or counselors to examine the roots of their children's disconcerting behavior or attitudes. They just react with gut feelings and family traditions.

Parenting Is a Unique Relationship

Parenting is a unique relationship in which parents are authorized by law and by God to protect, provide, nurture, and discipline their children. It is a special relationship, one in which the parent is fully responsible for the child in the early years and only a little less responsible as the child grows older. It requires enormous amounts of time, energy, and money. It requires tough love and tender affection, and there are many shades of grey in the middle. Parenting is challenging because every situation is complicated and varies from past situations. What works today may not work tomorrow, and the stakes are high, because the "success" or "failure" of a child directly impacts the good or bad reputation of the parents. What other relationship comes close to that kind of responsibility and intimacy?

Every Parent is a Role Model

Some people are not at all comfortable with being role models for kids, but parents are the role models for their children for better or for worse, like it or not. Parenting, then, should be more about controlling ourselves than controlling anyone else. Perfection may be out of reach, but striving for honesty and transparency will be incredibly helpful to children. Christopher DeVinck explains, "The more a parent points out things to their children, the more the children will take it upon themselves to select, identify, listen to, see, embrace. Life imitates life. Children do what adults do."[1]

Our kids, no matter the age, need us to be with them, explaining what makes one thing beautiful and another ugly, why one thing is important and the other trivial, and why this is quite right and that is all wrong. "With" is the key. A "with each other" relationship is what makes the world a better place, one person at a time, but this kind of relationship is not born of a few quick high-quality moments per day. It is born of quantity time and quality time. The sooner we embrace that, the better.

Parent Traps to Watch Out For
Many people fail to identify the kind of parent they want to be. They just do what seems best moment by moment, and the next thing they know, they find themselves regretting being too lenient, too strict, or too distant. Below are a few of the common traps that parents fall into.

The Friend
Perhaps the biggest trend in parenting is the role of best friend: supportive, kind, funny, sharing, generous, and cool. Being the best buddy trumps all other roles. Being cool and accepted by the child is paramount.

Cool parents are interested in all the details of the child's social life, wanting to know about all the boyfriends and girlfriends. They want to make certain that the child is on the right team, wearing exactly the right clothes, and attending the right events. In some cases, they dress and talk like the kids, trying to impress them. As time goes on, children learn that these parents can be controlled socially.

The Judge

The oldest parenting role is that of supreme ruler. This is the old-school mentality that a parent must dish out memorable punishments for every crime. This mindset is all about behavior modification, and it depends on setting up just the right rules, punishments, and rewards. This parent is typically tough and rarely tender.

Judges take great pride—sometimes to the point of bragging—in how strict they are in meting out punishments for poor behavior or attitude. Judges are certain that their children will not respond to anything but spankings, hot sauce on the tongue, lengthy groundings, or whatever they think is most clever in their penal system. The child rarely, if ever, gets hugs or praise unless some very high standard is met. The judge is hard to please.

The Distant Uncle

Perhaps the most common role is the parent that provides a house, food, clothes, transportation, and cable TV, but does not engage with the child on a personal level. This parent is like an out-of-town uncle: nice, supportive, but uninvolved in the kid's daily life.

Uncles give good gifts at Christmas, are fun to be around on vacation, and are decent family members, but they do not know much about the inner being of the child. In fact, the child's teachers and coaches know more about the child than they do. The child wishes for more but cannot see a path to greater closeness because the parent will not engage in talk or play.

The Helicopter

The overly involved helicopter parent has gotten headlines lately. He is so concerned about the safety and success of the child that failure is not an option. He hovers around the child and makes sure that she never fails or gets hurt in any way. He runs interference against anything that might upset the child. He is the rescuer. But in reality, he is an enabler. He is creating codependency.

The helicopter parent will do the child's homework if the child is crying about it. He will demand explanations from teachers for every low grade. Some will even fill out their teenagers' college applications. It is more important to the helicopter parent that his child be appreciative than independent, but the umbilical cord needs to be cut. The child needs to grow up to be independent, not codependent. An old Native American proverb says, "Do not prepare the path for the child. Prepare the child for the path and he will find his way."

Avoid the Extremes

There is no perfect balance, but a good balance can be crafted. Simply put, avoid the extremes. Do not be the most permissive, most cool, most involved, most strict, or most anything parent. Think of the Friend, the Judge, the Distant Uncle, and the Helicopter Parent as four corners of a boxing ring; you want to keep in the center of the ring, since the corners are where you get beaten. Extremes cause problems—usually in the form of resentful, rebellious teenagers.

Get Connected

It's no mystery that the best parents are the ones who are well connected with their children and offer support and guidance all along the way. They're the ones who care enough to say, "No, you can't do that, because I love you too much to let you settle for that kind of life." Good parenting is about being confident that you have a far higher calling than to just be a friend or dish out punishment. It is about being an authority who loves always and takes the time to guide and train a child to grow into an independent person. It is about being the one who plants love, truth, and hope into the mind of a child.

Ultimately, children are far less likely to engage in problem behaviors when they feel deeply loved, known, and respected by their parents. Author Danny Silk writes, "The goal isn't to get them to clean their room; it is to strengthen the connection to your heart. We will deal with the room, but if we lose the connection, we've lost the big stuff. We may win the battle, but we've lost the war."[2]

Parents, I invite you to lead your children wisely. Be the one who calls the shots, sets the agenda, and makes the tough choices. Be the strong one. Be the one who loves. Be the one who serves. Be the one who teaches. Be soft at some point every day, and yet be willing to be the tough cop when an authority is needed. Take pride in your attempts to be a strong, loving parent.

At times, parenting is the toughest job in the world, especially in those early years when it is so difficult to communicate with a hysterical three-year-old, or in the second toddlerhood of adolescence. And yet, once a healthy, loving, authoritative relationship is established, it is not so hard anymore. In fact, it is not only deeply satisfying, it can be fun.

All parents can be better than they once were. It is never too late.

WHAT GOT ME THROUGH THE EARLY YEARS

Like those of my wife and many of my best friends, my earliest childhood experiences were sweet. But when I was nine, my family life spun out of control, and I was fifteen when things settled down again. For me, the middle school years were pretty rough. They felt like survival. The song "Better Things" by Andy Gullahorn[1] is the story of my childhood; it sums up my inner life as a very young man.

> Ten years old and tough as nails
> Out of my garage I came
> I'd ride my Huffy down these trails
> Almost every day
>
> Sometimes I'd ride for the sport
> Sometimes I'd ride for the fun
> But mostly I would ride my bike
> As a way to run
>
> And I'd ride my bike as far as it would go
> Take in all that damage had done
> Saying "I won't go back until I know

That I can trade these for some
Better things to come."

There's no question in my mind
My mom and dad both love their son.
I wish that I could trade that love
To make them get along.

'Cause their angry words were thrown like knives
The wounds they left are here to stay
They thought I was safe from harm
As I went out to play

And I know those better things will come
And even if they don't
Instead of living life in fear
I'd rather live in hope

I took that Huffy years ago
To trade in for a mountain bike.
Now when I get the urge to go
I go with my wife.

I like to think I live and learn.
I'm learning love can be a ride uphill
'Cause I still feel the scars from knives they threw
And I guess I always will.

This song digs into the faded memories of my adolescence, which was a mostly confusing, sad time for me. The wounds have healed over the years. I love my parents, and I harbor no grudges for things that happened thirty years ago, but it is not possible for a child to pass through a parent's rocky marriage, divorce, remarriage, and another divorce unscathed.

It was especially hard for me from ten to fourteen. Before that, I had lived in a house with parents who did not like each other and with an older sister who was hurting, rebelling, and taking it out on us all. When I was ten, our parents divorced, which brought about stepparents, stepbrothers, and awkward travel from one house to the other. My mom's second marriage two years later was a rebound and did not go well for any of us. When I was fourteen the bulk of the chaos was over, but I was largely on my own, the man of the house.

Fortunately, I had some powerful healing agents.

My Bike

Until the age of ten, I lived on a seventy-acre farm outside of St. Louis. We had a long driveway with a huge speed bump in the middle, and I would walk my black Huffy dirt bike from the garage to the top of the big hill where the asphalt met a cattle guard and turned into gravel. From there I would launch-pedal my bike down the blacktop drive, rumble over the wooden bridge, coast past our old brick house, jump the speed bump, and sail on to the end of the driveway. I would backpedal to a rubber-reducing halt right at the entrance to our farm, where the bright red "Elm Farm" sign hung over the old wrought-iron mailbox. I was a frequent flyer on that rocket ride, especially when the house was full of tension.

Tall Trees

Our farm had the best trees. I'd climb a twenty-foot pine tree near the house, getting sap all over my hands to get to the tippy top. It would sway in the wind and I would hold on for life. I would climb the massive oak near the barn at the top of the hill, too, and hide for hours, making new routes up and down its thick branches. Nobody, not even my sisters, had any idea where I was. I would often go there just as the fighting was getting ugly, but I was not hiding as much as I was playing; and while I was playing, I was processing, which often bordered on prayer. Richard

11

Louv, author of *The Last Child in the Woods*, says, "Given a chance, a child will bring the confusion of the world to the woods, wash it in the creek, turn it over to see what lives on the unseen side of that confusion."[2] I was doing exactly that.

Sports

Another source of healing for me was playing competitive sports, where I could lose myself in the game and bond with my teammates and coaches. I swam on a swim team with kids of all ages, played baseball on a competitive traveling team, and played basketball on a select team and practiced a lot in the driveway and with friends before school. Later, I played high school football and basketball and ran on the track team.

Playing sports was instrumental in keeping me out of trouble, because when the going got tough, I had a healthy distraction and an outlet to blow off steam. I had a community and a sense of purpose, and my coaches and teammates were my role models for hard work, discipline, and sportsmanship—not always *good* role models, but ones that forced me to deal with conflict in a safe place. Experiencing success on those teams gave me a sense of self-esteem that I would not have had otherwise.

School and Camp

Although my mother was overwhelmed with raising three kids on her own and rebuilding her life after the divorce, she found ways to get me into schools and summer camps with teachers, coaches, and counselors who provided outstanding examples of manhood. From them, I learned strength, intelligence, self-control, love, service, excellence, and humility.

My own father was not around much, but I always knew that he loved and supported me, and I grew up with a fairly healthy amount of support and guidance, just not in the nuclear-family sort of way. Tuition money does not buy surrogate parents, but it can certainly provide a boost, and most kids need all the help they can get. My teachers, coaches, and counselors filled in the gaps of my broken family, and they're one of the main reasons I am a middle school educator now.

Faith in God

Of all the things that helped me get through the hard times of my middle school years, my Christian faith was key. It began at Vacation Bible School at the local Presbyterian church, where my mom sent me to keep me busy during spring break. When I heard the stories of Jesus in detail, I was inspired to live a life beyond myself. And when my counselors explained that I was a young man with problems, living in a world full of problems, but also part of a larger, better story of life, I fully understood that. No questions there. When they explained the good-news story of Jesus, I was on board. At ten, I understood it and embraced it.

We did not go to church much, but I did go to a Christian athletic camp every summer. When I was twelve, I watched my camp counselors live out their faith with love for others and great enthusiasm for life for a solid month. It was a good example of how seeing a sermon is always better than hearing one. They inspired me, more with deeds than with words, to seek a Christian life and live for more than myself. From then on, I could process my life with a deep sense of purpose. I could see my life as a story of redemption in which every trouble had profound purpose. By the start of high school, my faith was solid and growing. It was no longer just a Sunday morning thing.

I could not have grown up well without my own faith and the community of believers who helped me understand my life. Faith helped me deal with the pain in my heart and confusion in my mind. It still does.

Making Peace with My Adolescence

In spite of the pain that permeated my early adolescence, I do not look back on those rough years with resentment. So much has been redeemed in the thirty years since. At this point, I love my parents, and I very rarely think much about my childhood troubles. Through the grace of God and the love of many people over time, I have healed. As Henry Nouwen says, I am now a "wounded healer" in my role as husband, father, and middle school teacher.

Without the suffering, I would not have made an oath to myself at the age of ten to be a great husband and father when I grew up. Without the trouble, I would not have earned the empathy and resilience it takes to live my life now. I could not deal with all of my daughter's severe special needs if it were not for the deepening that took place in me during my teens.

I needed help in those vulnerable years, and by the grace of God, I got it from a wide variety of people who influenced me to be a better man and to help others do the same.

So What?

My story is pretty common for my generation, the children of the Baby Boomers. Most of us were children of divorce, but even those who were raised in intact families were often deprived of their parents' time and guidance, even as they were spoiled with material goods. As a result, we are trying to be more involved, more intentional, and more thoughtful about our own parenting practices. We want to raise our children in a better way, but we do not have the role models we need. We remember the Huxtable family from *The Cosby Show*, but there's nothing like it on TV anymore. We look to the experts, but they seem to contradict each other at every turn. So we parent the best we can, without much guidance, just as we grew up—largely on our own.

In his book *How Children Succeed,* Paul Tough explains the importance of a loving early childhood to the success of a young adult. His research shows that a child who is well-loved and supported will typically fare much better in life than one who experiences some form of trauma, such as the death of a sibling or the daily stress of poverty. He goes into great detail about the long-term, negative effects of too much stress in the early years, but he also offers hope for those who have endured great hardship in childhood.

> We now know that early stress and adversity can get under a child's skin, where it can cause damage that lasts a lifetime. But there is also some positive news in this research. It turns out that there is a particularly effective antidote to the ill effects of early stress, and it comes not from the pharmaceutical companies or the early-childhood educators but from parents. Parents and other caregivers who are able to form close, nurturing relationships with their children can foster resilience in them that protects them from many of the worst effects of a harsh early environment.[3]

This is welcome news to parents who have a measure of hope and a lot of questions: it is not too late to be a good parent. With a lot of help, love, support, and guidance, young teenagers can rebound with great resilience. I hope and pray that this book will be helpful, because one thing is certain: our kids will not do a good job of raising themselves.

FAMILIES MATTER

Two American families live on the same street, both living the American dream. Their Christmas cards are handsome. All their kids are college bound. Their marriages are stable, and they are in the midst of meeting their career and material goals. But there is a difference that only their very closest friends and family might recognize. Let's look a little more closely at them.

Meet the Davis family. Jim is an engineer who works long hours but makes time to go to all his kids' athletic events. He is a Boy Scout leader, a deacon at church, and a really nice guy by all accounts. His wife, Sue, works part-time as a nurse at the local children's hospital in addition to raising three teenagers. Jack, sixteen, plays three competitive sports and gets mostly As in school. He plays guitar in a garage band and loves to race his dirt bike with his friends on the weekends. Sally, fourteen, is a good student and a truly outstanding gymnast who travels a lot on the weekends for competitions. When she's home, she likes to go to the mall or the movie theater to be with her friends as much as possible. Jimmy, twelve, is interested in everything; he has dozens of hobbies. He plays select soccer, is a Boy Scout, and still manages good grades. All in all, the Davises are active, productive, and very busy. They seem content with life and get along well with all kinds of people. They are good neighbors, but they are not home much.

Now, meet the Rodriguez family next door. Lewis is also an engineer, and Donna works part-time at the elementary school their three teenage kids attended. Josh, Jonny, and Claire are seventeen, fifteen, and thirteen, respectively. They are above-average students, but do not excel in sports or the arts. After dinner every night, they like to watch movies together, so they built a family theater and a ping pong arena in the basement. Whenever possible, they get away to Grandpa's cabin on a lake, where they do a lot of fishing, waterskiing, swimming, cliff jumping, and reading. Lately, at night, they've been playing some animated games of Texas Hold'em; Mom is the best bluffer of the bunch. Their neighbors miss them when they are gone at the cabin because they are a fun-loving family.

So what is the difference? It is subtle but powerful: the difference is *with*. One family lives *with* each other, while the other is on the run, often in opposite directions. The Rodriguezes play with each other, hang out with each other, and eat with each other more often than not. The Davises, however, are not with each other much, except in the car en route to an activity. One family is a team, while the other is a bunch of individuals. The Davises may appear to be a tight family, but they are not. They each have their individual lives, full of their own favorite activities; they freely pursue their own happiness, free from the inconveniences of too much family time.

In the ABC sitcom *The Middle*[1], the Heck family is a very middle-class family in middle America, and their family situation is right down the middle—not truly dysfunctional, but far from ideal. One evening, Frankie (the mom) witnesses the loving bond of her neighbor's kids, then goes home to see the total lack of bonding in her own children. They are all under the same roof, but they are not connected to each other. The kids are each pursuing their own dreams: Brick pursues books, Axel pursues sports and girls, and Sue pursues cross-country or whatever fad is her latest obsession. When the parents see the weak bonds in their home, they decide to do something about it. Of course, the show gets ridiculous after that, but at least they are trying. It is an epiphany that most families never have and even fewer families attempt to act on.

So what exactly is the big deal about spending family time together? Well, it's *not* a big deal if parents want to teach their kids that life is all about pursuing their own interests and goals. But family bonding is crucial to healthy child development, especially in the early years.

Everybody needs a family or some kind of tight-knit community to fit into. Every person needs to belong, and it is in that place of belonging that we must learn to give and take and work together. The family unit doesn't have to be a traditional two-parent one with two kids and a dog, but it does need to be a group that has an identity, so children can verify and validate their own identities. Being part of a tribe is crucial to growing up well. We all need to belong to a family, long after we leave home to start our own families.

The Marines, who describe themselves as "The few, the proud, the Marines," demonstrate that if a little bonding goes a long way, then a lot of bonding goes all the way. They know how to give young men an unparalleled sense of pride and solidarity of purpose, and their motto, *Semper fidelis*, means "always faithful." Ask a Marine if he will fall on a grenade to save his fellow Marines, and he won't hesitate to say "Yes, sir"—and he's probably just saying "sir" to be polite, since you aren't a Marine. They know all about hard work, toughness, loyalty, and sacrifice.

Can your family teach that kind of solidarity? Do you feel deeply connected to each other? When people talk about your family, what do they say?

I know a family that is a team and has an identity. The kids all know how to act because Mom and Dad let them know all the time. When the little kids start whining without just cause, Dad barks out, "Hey, Millers! Is that what Millers do? No, Millers do not whine. Millers use words." Yes, he's a high school coach, and that is probably why the family operates so much like a team. Dad knows that winners are not made in isolation, and he knows kids will perform better for a coach and teammates who care about them.

Even in an individual sport like swimming, wrestling, or cross-country, the best performers have teammates and coaches who act as a family and provide identity, purpose, and support every day. They are a loving, loyal, tough bunch of kids because their parents are teaching and training them how. Family identity, like team spirit, is no accident. It is an intentional set of traditions designed to create meaningful relationships. It matters that kids grow up with parents, stepparents, and grandparents who not only provide for them and encourage them, but also work with, play with, lounge with, eat with, and joke with them daily.

Joann, my dental hygienist for over ten years, is another example of a parent who has created a team in her home. She's a single mom of three boys—big strapping athletic kids. Instead of putting them on every competitive sports team possible, she tried to strike a balance to keep the family together as much as possible. They had their share of basketball games and practices to attend, but they also went camping, played cards, did chores, watched movies, and built a family life together. Her small budget and small house were not sources of stress for the boys; instead, they learned to accept the fact that they would usually be doing things together. As time went on, the boys earned good grades and eventually went off to play basketball and go to colleges far away. It was not easy for Joann or the boys to be apart, but as time went on, she got remarried and the boys found wives. They are still a very tight family and go on family vacations together annually. They still belong to each other, and it is because they were with each other in those critical early years and shared their lives as a team. The kids grew up very well because family was first.

Take an honest look at your family. Are you *with* each other, intentionally building a family that is a tightly knit team? Adolescents require more than an individual can provide. This will become more apparent as this book develops. It takes a village to raise a young man or woman well, but it all starts in the home, with a team approach.

DEFINING ADOLESCENCE

I swim in a sea of adolescence. As a parent of two middle school students, and as a middle school teacher, I am surrounded by young teenagers. When I walk into the seventh-grade hallway at 7:30 in the morning to begin my workday, I sometimes wonder what I'm doing in this jungle of young primates. Why do I choose to teach pre-people? Teaching is hard enough, but this . . .

But other times, I pass by the laughing girls and the gangly boys, and I wonder what will happen on that day's adventure. Because if there is just one way to describe middle school students, it is *dynamic*. Nothing stays the same in the life of a middle school kid or class. This anonymous poem by an eighth-grade student describes the paradoxes of middle-school life:

> What is a middle schooler,
> I was asked one day.
> I knew what he was . . .
> but what should I say?
> He is noise and confusion.
> He is silence that is deep.

He is sunshine and laughter,
or a cloud that will weep.
He is swift as an arrow.
He is a waster of time.
He wants to be rich,
but cannot save a dime.
He is rude and nasty.
He is polite as can be.
He wants parental guidance,
but fights to be free.
He is aggressive and bossy.
He is timid and shy.
He knows all the answers,
but still will ask "why?"
He is awkward and clumsy.
He is graceful and poised.
He is ever changing,
but do not be annoyed.
What is a middle schooler,
I was asked one day.
He is the future unfolding.
Do not stand in his way.[1]

Disconnection

Mark Twain once said, "When I was a boy of fourteen, my father was so ignorant I could hardly stand to have the old man around. But when I got to be twenty-one, I was astonished at how much the old man had learned in seven years." There is egotism in every adolescent, and it reveals itself in all sorts of unpredictable ways. It drives most adults crazy because so often the kid's attitude screams, "I know best! I will prevail, in spite of you!" But there is also sweetness, vulnerability, honesty, and a host of other wonderful characteristics in that young person.

Making a connection is the first step towards influencing young teenagers. Parents can make connections with even the most surly, disruptive, and annoying adolescents, but it may be a slow process. Spending some one-on-one time with them will usually soften them, but it may take a few weeks to see much change. However, without a connection, parents will have little to no influence.

There are very few kids out there who will continue to defy an adult who takes the time to listen and communicate with them. They'll usually open up before long and reveal a much more complex situation than was first apparent. The kids who stay closed-up are hurting and in need of attention, especially from a caring adult. One conversation will not change the entire life of a child, but it can sometimes save them from doing or saying something that will cause them a world of hurt. One conversation may be the thing they consider later when they are ready to make a change. And enough caring conversations and nonverbal support from adults can certainly change a child's young-adult life. Connection can change a child's life in profound ways.

In order to connect with our early adolescents, it is important to understand them to some degree. We must have appropriate expectations of what they are—not children anymore, but not fully adult yet, either.

What Exactly is Early Adolescence?
Early adolescence is a dynamic time of transformation that spans the fourth to eighth grades and ages ten through fourteen. Just stand in a fourth-grade hallway during passing time, then go visit an eighth-grade hallway. They are so alike and yet so different. The kids are exiting childhood and entering young adulthood, so they are ten going on fourteen, or fourteen going on eighteen.

Early adolescents are trying desperately to understand themselves, their world, and where they fit in. They are searching for meaning and value in their lives, often unsuccessfully. They often struggle with identity issues, weak self-esteem, and peer pressure. In addition, they are struggling to keep up with their academic, athletic, artistic, and other activities. It is a time of turmoil for some, and for others it is a time of wonder. For most, it is both an exciting adventure into a larger world and an anxious time of uncertainty. It is a paradox.

Some people see adolescents as alien life forms, but the universe does not abduct sweet little eleven-year-old children and replace them with aliens that are neither children nor adults. Adolescence is a natural stage of life, and early adolescence is a brief period marked by dramatic transformation. Remember this: most people do not change much after age fifteen. The most dramatic change is usually in early adolescence.

What does it mean to grow up?
What is the goal of adolescence, beyond mere survival?

In my English class we read several coming-of-age novels. In one of those novels, our discussions focuses on exactly what it means to grow up, and I kick it off by giving the students definitions from two unlikely sources. The first is just a blog comment by someone named Sarge927 who wrote:

> A person "grows up" when he/she learns to take responsibility for his/her own actions and stops behaving as if the world revolves around him/her. Many people never truly grow up because they constantly blame others for everything "bad" that has happened in their lives, or they expect everyone and everything in their world to conform to their point of view. People who are grown up will suck it up and pay the price if they get caught breaking the law, even if it's just a speeding ticket, while those who are not grown up will try to find any and every way to weasel out of it. People who are grown up will give and don't

always expect to get, but those who are not grown up will always ask "What's in it for me?"[2]

The second is from Ann Landers, who defined growing up as the achievement of maturity:

Maturity is the ability to do a job whether you are supervised or not; finish a job once it is started; carry money without spending it and be able to bear an injustice without wanting to get even.

Maturity is the ability to control anger and settle differences without violence.

Maturity is patience. It is the willingness to postpone immediate gratification in favor of the long-term gain.

Maturity is perseverance, the ability to sweat out a project or a situation in spite of heavy opposition and discouraging setbacks.

Maturity means dependability, keeping one's word, coming through in a crisis. The immature are masters of the alibi. They are confused and disorganized. Their lives are a maze of broken promises, former friends, unfinished business and good intentions that somehow never materialized.[3]

I urge you to start a similar conversation about maturity with your own children. Write down the characteristics you want your children to have by the time they are eighteen. When you have a long list, separate it into two or three columns: nonnegotiables and hopefuls, maybe, and define for your family a common set of values.

For extra credit, create a family crest, a collage, or a wall of photographs that illustrates your family's most important values. If you have an artist in the family, commission him to create something meaningful and beautiful. Pay him well and post his work in a prominent place. Or perhaps a mission statement is something that would work for your family. Anything that sets the values and vision of the family will be a good thing for everybody.

Some Professional Advice

The real question is how to help these confused young people get to a place of grown-up responsibility and empathy. Clearly, maturing is a long process. It is Crockpot cooking. Change is measured in years, not months, and it is crucial to keep that in mind. We cannot expect our twelve-year-olds to act like twenty-year-olds, but we can expect them to become more mature each year. For many middle school kids, twelve is an age of regression to toddlerhood, but this should not be acceptable.

My middle school principal, Steve Hall, offers this advice to parents of incoming seventh graders (twelve-year-olds):

Top Ten Things You Should Know About Your Middle School Student 4

10. Each student has one compelling mission each day: Avoid embarrassment! It is true that most students believe everyone is watching them at all times. Each student believes that a misplaced word, a stumble in the hallway, or a failure to meet the unwritten rules of middle school culture— though, in reality, they are unknown to anyone— will be seen and remembered forever by all classmates. Parents, don't take it personally if they don't want to hug in public anymore.

9. Although all outward evidence suggests otherwise, you are a very important person to your child, and your child feels more secure and valued when you care enough to talk with them about anything and everything. Don't let the rolling eyes or mock disdain deter you. It's one of those unwritten rules they have to follow as teenagers.

8. You will require a hazmat suit and gas mask to handle the unique aromas coming from young teenagers. The truth is that kids are self-conscious about the changes that create these issues. It's a time of a great deal of change in height, weight, and appearance. Your child needs a proper diet, plenty of sleep, and good hygiene. Be courageous as parents and talk about these changes. The more you talk about them, the easier the discussions will become.

7. Your child pretends you are Nero, but, in reality, you are a hero! Over and over again, both in polls and interviews, teens consistently say they highly value and cherish their parents. Just remember that they don't need a pal, but they also don't need a prison warden. They need someone to emulate and trust. They need someone who is looking beyond the mess to provide them with perspective and strength.

6. When it comes to middle school kids, mood changes can be predicted by nothing! If you haven't noticed a few mood changes and mood swings in your child yet, just wait, because they're likely coming! Simply put, kids are attempting to handle all of the changes, social uncertainty, and awkwardness of maturation, and it can be a bit overwhelming at times. Your child will need your patience, understanding, and direction. The best advice is this: Pray for your children and pray with your children on a daily basis.

5. Apparently, middle school kids are all equipped to become Supreme Court justices. You will be shocked to find out how often you are wrong, according to your child. I imagine from a middle school child's perspective that it's a wonder adults can function well in this world. The truth is that

middle school children feel a strong pull to be independent and adultlike thinkers. However, their thinking is characterized by overanalysis and is often followed by a definitive black-and-white conclusion to the matter. In some cases, their conclusions fly in the face of a parent's perspective simply so they can test what it means to be independent. Encourage, nurture, guide, and value your child's growth in this area. Some studies have concluded that 75% of all fourteen-year-olds are still primarily operating in a concrete stage of learning. Abstract thinking is emerging at this age, but oftentimes in an awkward way.

4. There is so much diversity in development among this age group. An eighth-grade student might be six foot three and his best friend five foot four; some students might interact socially like elementary school students, while others sound more like high school students. Emotional and intellectual responses to the same issue can vary greatly. The bottom line: never, ever, ever compare your child's development to that of another middle school student. Your job is to help your child grow in a manner that promotes maturity, that considers his or her unique interests and tastes, and that equips him or her to manage and function effectively (I didn't say "perfectly"!) in the various settings in which he or she will work and live.

3. The middle school motto for living: "There is no I in TEAM, but there is M and E . . . ME!" Egocentric is a word that perfectly fits this age group. Everything relates back to the child from his perspective. I would offer two pieces of advice. First, help your son or daughter better understand the world around him or her, the great

needs of others outside of his or her own experience, and how to think of others first. Second, be patient. Our children are mini versions of us. Aren't we daily struggling with a bit of egocentrism ourselves?

2. Your child believes he or she is the only one who has not traveled to Tahiti for spring vacation. This is a subtle variation on the theme of egocentrism. Here is the point: your child's perception is his or her reality. A middle school child's problems don't always seem big to us, because our age and experience allow us to live in a bigger world. However, your child lives in a much smaller world, so his or her concerns are truly very big to him or her. Your child may very well believe that his or her particular situation is the only one of its kind. Respect and listen to your child's concerns, and move him or her gently towards reality.

1. Nothing says I love you like a noogie! The love languages and social-interaction styles of this age group are very unusual. Boys' affections and appreciation are best communicated physically. Play and physicality seem to be at the core of true relationship-building. Dads, this is why there is a growing desire in your son to wrestle you. Moms, this is why your boy no longer sweetly hugs you, but wants to impress you with a giant bear hug. Girls are a bit different. It seems that at the core of all great female middle school relationships is drama! It appears that girls believe life is an exciting adventure.

Despite the peculiarities of this age group, which are many and sometimes intimidating, in the final analysis, they need you, want you, and love you. Make a commitment to understand this stage of life. Know your child. Don't dread these years, but make it your goal to love this time together. Love the experience. Love your child! This can and should be a wonderful time of life for both you and your child to grow together.

It's a Wonderful Stage of Life

Adolescence is a stage many people miss out on because they are either looking back at the cute elementary school years or forward to the more glamorous high school years.

Trace Adkins sings a song called "You're Gonna Miss This"[5] about how we need to cherish the beauty in each stage of life. In his deep, grandfatherly voice, he sings:

> She was starin' out the window of their SUV,
> Complainin', sayin', "I can't wait to turn eighteen."
> She said, "I'll make my own money and I'll make my own rules.
> Momma, put the car in park out there in front of the school."
> And she kissed her head, and said, "I was just like you.
>
> You're gonna miss this
> You're gonna want this back
> You're gonna wish these days
> Hadn't gone by so fast
> These are some good times
> So take a good look around
> You may not know it now
> But you're gonna miss this."

A lot of people look back on their early teen years with disdain. For many of us, survival seems like the only feasible goal for early adolescence. In fact, many counselors will essentially say, "If you can just get through the middle school years without deep emotional scars, then you are golden." But I do not subscribe to that philosophy. I have seen many great families enjoy these years as much or more than the elementary years.

I believe that these last few years of childhood should be cherished. I also believe that connecting with children and guiding them into young adulthood is as exciting as it is important. It will not be easy, but doing great things never is. It will require a great deal of time, energy, thought, prayer, and support from others to help a child grow up well, but these investments will pay off with a lifetime of rich rewards for parent, child, and community. After all, in just a few years, your child will be driving away with new friends to go on new adventures. And then a few years later, she will move out to live in a different home or dorm room with other people who will be like family to her. And then she will fall in love and marry someone. The decade will go by much faster than you think. For me, it feels like a fast-moving train. My goal is to invest in my children now, while they are still moldable and under my protective care, so that we may look back with fondness and look ahead with hope.

THE POWER OF CONNECTION

"My dad doesn't get me" is a phrase thought far too often by young teenagers, who wonder why their parents spend less and less time with them each year. For parents, connecting and staying connected with children is more challenging the older they get. Nevertheless, there is no greater way to help a child grow up well inside and out than to be with them and to get them.

Many children are fortunate enough to experience love from their moms and dads and other significant adults in ways that give them a solid sense of acceptance and worth. They grow up knowing that they are loved as is and that someone is very proud of them. Unfortunately, many other kids strive for a blessing that they never quite get from Mom or Dad or another adult. They feel that their parents love them when . . . if . . . as long as . . . And children know that conditional love is not real love. They struggle under a love that is either conditional or unexpressed or both. As a result, they are not free to give and receive love as well as they need to.

In their book *The Blessing,* Gary Smalley and John Trent explain how important the family blessing is to every young person. "The family blessing not only provides people a much-needed sense of personal acceptance, it also plays an important part in protecting and even freeing them to develop intimate relationship. The best defense against a child's longing for imaginary acceptance is to provide him or her with genuine acceptance." You just cannot go wrong with giving your children honest affirmation at home. "No matter your age, the approval of your parents affects how you view yourself and your ability to pass that approval on to your children, spouse and friends. This is vital to your self-esteem and emotional well-being."[1]

For some adults, making connections with children comes naturally. My wife, for instance, has no trouble with it. She is a trusting, optimistic extrovert. Even when she was a child, she would connect with people and stay connected; she is a lover of people—always has been, always will be. Every family, church, and school needs these people to create an atmosphere of goodwill toward children. But not everybody finds it so easy. Many of us were not raised by people who expressed their love clearly, so we don't have a good example to go by. I, for example, am an introvert, and I find it difficult to connect with some young people. I am not a youth-group leader type who can hang out with kids for hours, gabbing and joking. I am a teacher. I am good with kids in the classroom, but making connections with some kids is sheer work at times, and often very awkward. Sometimes I succeed, sometimes I fail, but it doesn't come easily to me.

Fortunately, every adult, even the most introverted among us, can connect with a kid in some authentic way. It boils down to four essential elements: words, experiences, touch, and gifts. It is not any more complicated than that, and the real beauty is that you don't have to be a master of all the elements; in fact, it would be unusual if you were. The following is loosely based on Gary Chapman's five love languages.

Constructive Words

Parents reap the results of the words they sow in their children. The Bible says, "Death and life are in the power of the tongue, and those who love it will eat its fruits" (Proverbs 18:21). This tells us to speak words of construction, not destruction. Now, this does not mean that you cannot speak negatively, but it means that you must be building up rather than tearing down.

For example, if a son speaks horribly, cursing his mother, then his father should speak with strength about how very wrong that is, and teach him how to make it right. It might sound like this: "I want you to listen very carefully to me and take these words to heart. I don't ever—and I mean *ever*—want to hear you speak like that to your mother, or to any other woman, for that matter. You are not that kind of person. I know you, and this is not who you are. You made a mistake—like we all do—and you can now try to fix it and learn from it. When you are ready, and it may take a while, you can apologize to your mother." So, there you have a negative reinforcement (an unpleasant confrontation) for a negative behavior, but the ultimate purpose is to build up the boy and to empower him to do right next time.

Mundane situations like riding in the car or watching TV provide countless opportunities for expressing your pleasure and pride in your child with constructive words. Just having a conversation that includes laughter can be a bonding experience. Smalley and Trent provide dozens of testimonials from people who were greatly blessed by their parents:

- My parents would always make sure I knew why I was being disciplined.

- Now that I'm an adult, I appreciate how my father taught me to communicate with him. That has helped me know how to talk with my husband now that I'm married.

- My parents prayed for me out loud, even when I didn't feel like I deserved it.

- My father would ask to talk to each of us kids personally when he called from a trip.

- I never felt as if I had to perform to gain my father's approval.

- They would let me explain my side of the story.

- They were willing to admit when they were wrong and say "I'm sorry."

- My father let me share in his failures as well as his successes.

A teacher friend of mine polled her sixth-grade students about what their parents do really well in raising them. Their responses can teach us how to interact with our kids:

- I can tell my mom anything (good or bad), and she loves me no matter how annoying I am.

- When I play sports, my parents cheer me on no matter if I win or lose or play well or not. They don't criticize me.

- My parents listen to me before grounding me or something.

- My parents are kind and gentle with me. They don't say bad things about me.

- They don't yell and cuss at me or anything, like some other parents do.

Just Ask

Asking questions provides great opportunities to show children that you truly care about who they are and what they are really thinking. Almost any question will do. Just be prepared for one-word answers, especially from the boys. You may have to prod a little, and you will have to listen carefully. Sometimes it's not easy to get the conversation started, but nothing great comes with ease. The following are questions for parents and non-parents. Pick what seems appropriate for you.

- How's it going today? What's up this morning?

- What did you do this past weekend? What was the best and worst part of it?

- What do you want to do this weekend? Anything fun or unusual?

- What do you want to do during Christmas break? (or whatever break is upcoming)

- What sport are you playing this season? How's that going? What position do you play? What team? Who is on that team that I might know? What's your coach like?

- Do you (want to) play a musical instrument?

- What's your favorite hobby now? Tell me about that. What do you like about it?

- Who are the friends you like to hang out with? Who would you go to for help? Who is the funniest kid you know? What makes him or her so funny?

- What area are you most successful in? Do you like that? Do you think you might do more with that later? Is there a career in that area that you could pursue?

- What's your favorite music, band, movie, food, restaurant, sport to watch, sport to play, athlete, TV show, vacation . . .

Caring Touch

Parents are great at touching infants and toddlers in the age of snuggling, but after those early years, many stop hugging their kids. The physical distance can grow quite cold as the years stretch on and electronic devices are wedged in between parent and child.

Smalley and Trent offer some more words of advice from young adults who were parented well:

- We would hold hands together when we said grace; then when we finished, we would squeeze the person's hand next to us three times, which stood for "I love you."

- We were often spontaneously getting hugged, even apart from a task or chore.

- My mom used to rub my legs after cheerleading practice.

- Even when I was very overweight in high school, my parents still made me feel attractive.

- When I wrecked my parents' car, my father's first reaction was to hug me and let me cry, instead of yelling at me.

- My father would put his arm around me at church and let me lay my head on his shoulder.

- They would look me in the eyes when they said something nice.

And more from the sixth-graders in my friend's classroom:

- My dad wrestles with me to cheer me up.

- My dad and I play catch, and we play soccer. He is pretty rough, which is fun.

- We watch movies on the couch and snuggle under blankets together.

- They got me a dog, and we hug it a lot.

Clearly, the need for touch is real. You just have to find ways that are appropriate and comfortable. And perhaps Mom is more huggy than Dad, but that is just fine. Dad can give high fives or pats on the back—whatever works for him. And pets can provide the touch that kids need. A friend of mine once told me that the key to preventing his girls from seeking the affection of teenage boys was to make sure they had dogs and cats in the house—and if he could afford it, he'd buy them horses, just to be safe.

More great sources of touch are the family prayer and the goodnight hug. In our home, we hold hands for prayer at dinner and at bedtime, and we always give hugs at bedtime. This tradition ensures that our kids get at least some kind of meaningful touch every day, even when my wife and I are exhausted and distracted. Traditions often force great things to happen.

Shared Experiences
If a family is going to survive in a culture that seems intent upon tearing it apart, it must become a strong team. In order to become a strong team, parents must share their lives, their stories, and their wisdom with their kids.

It has been said that the family that camps together stays together. Everybody pitches in to pack, set up camp, cook, clean, and go hiking and swimming. Everything is a shared experience that can lead to laughing, arguing, negotiation, and lots of stories. And in the process, there is real bonding.

But camping is not the only way for a family to bond. Plenty of studies support the idea the families who eat together stay together. Michael J. Fox said it best: "The oldest form of theater is the dinner table. It's got five or six people, new show every night, same players. Good ensemble; the people have worked together a lot. I heard at a parenting seminar that the best place to reduce stress and boost confidence in children is to set aside a regular time together at the dinner table. I shall eat with my boy!" It doesn't matter whether the food is home-cooked or the conversation is deep and meaningful. Any old meal and any old topic of conversation will do, and sometimes magic will happen. Someone will tell a great story, and everyone will laugh until milk comes out of someone's nose. Someone will share something heartbreaking, and someone else will sympathize. Someday, someone will ask a tough question like "Why does God let bad things happen to good people?" and the whole group will debate. Mom will tell stories about her mother's childhood during the Great Depression that amaze everyone. Magic will not happen every night or every week, but the chances multiply every time you sit down together. And it is a perfect time for family prayer, which can bring its own magic.

In addition to the daily traditions of meals, prayers, and favorite TV shows, sharing your kids' interests is perhaps the best way to connect. My son is a soccer fanatic. He loves to play, watch, and talk about it. I grew up despising soccer, deeming it a boring sport with not enough scoring and the ridiculous rule of no hands, but I embrace it now because it lets me support my son. I've learned about Manchester United, Chelsea, Newcastle, and the other

Premier League teams in Europe. We take a twenty-four-hour trip to Kansas City every summer to watch their pro team, Kansas City Sporting, play in their awesome new stadium. I bought a new camera so I can take action shots of my son and his friends at their games. I have grown to like soccer, but more importantly, I have connected with my son. Does this make me a hero? No. I enjoy it. But I am a hero to him sometimes anyway, and that is priceless.

Another way to connect with kids is to take them on a new adventure, especially one that involves food. Last winter, I forced my son to go with my wife and me to look for bald eagles near one of their nesting places along the Mississippi River. He wanted to sleep late on "his Saturday," but we convinced him that he could sleep in the afternoon and that we could make it fun, one way or another. We promised him a good lunch (at least as good as Chik-fil-A)—which didn't help his attitude all that much at 7:30 a.m., but by 8:00, we were talking in the car about all sorts of things and laughing. At nine, we saw a bald eagle swoop down and land in a field within fifty yards of us. We travelled along roads, bridges, and rivers through small towns that we had never seen before and ate a great lunch at a country restaurant with fantastic raspberry cobbler. In the end, it was a good time, a good memory, and a good relationship-builder, even though he would have never chosen to do it on his own.

Experience educates children in ways that TV and video games cannot. Shared experiences will yield more than memories and knowledge; they will often lead to meaningful conversations about life, and that is where wisdom flows.

So, take a kid fishing. Pack her favorite snacks and some good bait. (Worms work.) Take a kid to a ballgame and buy him whatever snacks he wants. Take pictures. Buy souvenirs. Just get out there and do something memorable together. Take your child to her favorite restaurant and tell her she can have anything on the menu. Go bowling. Try laser tag. Go-karts. Whatever. Just do something.

But if you want the most bang for your buck, take your kids and their friends camping. It is a guaranteed memory-maker.

Meaningful Gifts

For some kids, nothing says I love you like a well-thought-out gift. This does not require much, if any, money, but it does require some thinking about what the child would like and how to make it personal—maybe with an encouraging card, a monogram, or an engraved message. Let the gift show that you know your child's personality and preferences. For example, I just bought my daughter a pink rhinestone bracelet for no particular occasion. She loves it because she loves pink, bracelets, and sparkles, and it's just the right size for her tiny wrist. It cost me just twelve dollars, but it might as well have been made of diamonds, especially since it was totally unexpected. I don't need to spoil her with expensive gifts, but giving her a meaningful gift every now and then lets me show her that I know her well.

The day my son was born, I went to K-Mart to develop the pictures and to buy a few things. While I was there, I bought my son his first stuffed animal, a tiny Winnie the Pooh, and placed it in his crib when I got back to the hospital. A few year later, I explained to him the significance of that little bear and told him about his birthday and how happy I was that day. I spent no more than four dollars for that little bear, but it's a family heirloom now. On that same trip, I bought my wife a small silver heart on a simple silver chain for about twenty dollars. I thought its intricate, delicate design was pretty, and it just seemed right for her. To this day, when she wears it, we think of that important day in our life of love with each other. Gifts like these are meaningful to both the giver and receiver.

Over the years, I've been given many special gifts by friends and family members. In my office I have a set of shed antlers, a gift from a very good friend who taught me the beauty and technique of deer hunting; he gave them to me on the day he moved to Michigan, a sad moment for me. My grandfather gave me a gift of great value when he found out I was going to ask my long-time girlfriend to marry me: the engagement ring he'd designed and made specially for his fiancée back in the 1920s. The center stone had been a gift to him from his father, and my grandmother wore that ring for over fifty years as her treasured possession. Their marriage weathered many years, and the center stone had many scratches and a small nick in the side. I told my fiancée the whole story when I gave that ring to her in 1993, and twenty years later, it is her favorite possession. She wears it proudly every day and is often complimented on its unique design. That is a meaningful gift, not for its platinum and diamonds, but for its symbolism and story. Perhaps that old ring will be a gift to our grandson in another forty years.

Some of the best gifts can cost absolutely nothing. A few years ago, before my son and I went out of town for a few days, we hid about two dozen little sticky notes all over the house—in drawers, on mirrors, in books, and so forth. So, for all the days we were gone, my wife kept finding little notes that praised her cooking, her kindness, her hugs, and all the other little things we love about her. Yeah, she cried. Several times. And she kept every little note and taped them up inside a kitchen cabinet. I'm not sure they are ever coming down.

Get personal with your gift-giving. It is more powerful than you think, especially when you offer presents with caring words, touches, and experiences. Communication is the key. You have to say what you mean and mean what you say, and you have to be understood. Your children must get that you love them as is. Until your children

45

know you care for them deeply, unconditionally, they will not listen to your wise words of guidance. First things first: connect.

TAKING CARE OF YOURSELF

Whenever we flew with our small children, the flight attendant would look us in the eye and say, "Remember, you must be sure to give oxygen to yourself first before giving it to your child. Got it?" This was always a sobering reminder that in a crisis, it is the parent who must be well enough to be the rescuer. This truth transcends air travel: sacrifice has its limits.

Self-denial is an essential element of good parenting, but there is an important caveat: parents must take care of themselves in order to care for their children well. If the sacrifice is not sustainable for the long haul (eighteen years per child), then major problems may result. Every active, conscientious parent needs to know how to practice sustainable parenting.

Teachers, like many parents, are typically hard-working and self-sacrificing. They work overtime without pay because they believe that what they are doing is of vital importance to other people. Most teachers are on a mission, but they crash and burn regularly because of their physically, mentally, and emotionally demanding lifestyle. The high teacher burnout rate is one of the reasons for all the breaks in the school calendar. I have been guilty of not taking care of myself properly, getting sick often, becoming disillusioned, and burning out several times a year. I'm not proud of it.

Parents who expect too much of themselves face even graver consequences: parents who break down will neglect or hurt their kids, one way or another.

What all of us need to do, parents and teachers alike, is set more reasonable expectations and take better care of ourselves. We should strive to maintain excellent work practices, health routines, and attitudes so we can continue year after year. We need to work smarter, not harder—and smarter might mean working a lot less.

My wife and I have recurring discussions about what we can do to avoid burnouts and breakdowns. It is always a frustrating conversation, but a necessary one. Our life is full of nonnegotiable responsibilities, so there are no easy ways to be more efficient and carve out a little more downtime. The truth is that there are not a lot of options for us; we have one child with multiple disabilities, another with extracurricular activities, and two busy careers in education. However, we can't give up on trying to create a sustainable lifestyle, and we have found that a Sabbath is absolutely necessary for us. If we do not rest enough on Sunday, we will crash and burn.

Some people have extraordinarily difficult situations that are entirely beyond their control. Their lives are full of absolutely essential responsibilities that cannot be managed into more reasonable, happy situations. I have been there. My wife has been there. My mom has been there. Many of my friends have been there. You're in a tough spot when you feel like you can't make significant progress towards a better, more sane lifestyle, but giving up is never an option.

Sometimes you just have to keep doing the next thing until circumstances improve.

If Mama Ain't Happy . . .

Happy parents are far more likely than unhappy parents to have happy kids. This is a basic truth that is continually supported by research. Good parenting requires some inner happiness.

Donald Miller's book *A Million Miles in a Thousand Years* has a terrific chapter about happiness in which he refers to an episode of *60 Minutes* that I vividly recall seeing a few years ago. It was about the happiest people in the world: the good people of Denmark. "The reasons the Danes are so happy was this: they had low expectations. I'm not making that up. There is something in Denmark's culture that allows them to look at life realistically. They don't expect products to fulfill them or relationships to end all their problems."[1]

Another contributing factor the study turned up is the Danes' involvement in their local communities. More than any of the other developed nations in the study, people in Denmark were found to have a sense of equality and connectedness to each other. In fact, their values are so community-oriented that they have a popular government program that pays citizens to get involved in local recreational and social groups. As a result, they are far less competitive than Americans and more likely to weigh successes as a community, instead of as individuals in competition with one another. The Danes have reasonable expectations and are connected with their neighbors, which seems to make them significantly more content and happy than other nations. Donald Miller concludes his chapter with "When you stop expecting people to be perfect, you can like them for who they are. And when you stop expecting material possessions to complete you, you'd be surprised at how much pleasure you get in material possessions. And when you stop expecting God to end all your troubles, you'd be surprised how much you like spending time with God."[2]

If we adopt a more Danish approach to life, we might just be happier and be more effective in helping kids live healthy, happy lives. But "lower your expectations" is not exactly a winning slogan; some might even say it's un-American. It sounds like something Homer Simpson would teach Bart. However, in view of our hyperstressed American lifestyle, which is constantly shouting "More! More! More!," it makes sense. It is a call to embrace a more realistic, reasonable outlook.

Set Realistic Expectations

Disclaimer: The following passage is not for everyone. It is written for those who tend to be perfectionists. It is for those who often find themselves frustrated with their shortcomings. It is meant to encourage those who set high expectations but rarely meet their own standards. These things are in no particular order, and do not constitute a comprehensive list.

No Family Is Perfect

We should remember that imperfect people make imperfect families—so *every* family is dysfunctional, to some degree. However, the best families learn to love and support each other anyway.

While family life is one of the most important and rewarding of all human activities, it is also one of the most difficult. Marriage and family offer joy and purpose, but not perfection. They are rewarding, but they will not fill the void in your soul every day. Sadly, many parents relentlessly pursue the idea of the perfect family, and it's not healthy for them, their spouses, or their children.

The best way to develop a family is to love each other as is, without trying to change each other. Check yourself whenever you find yourself trying to change someone else. Manipulation is conditional love. It is a love killer.

God Doesn't Promise Perfection

Religion is often packaged for kids like a product for sale in this country. Youth groups and summer camps often teach that God will perfectly fill every need of the heart and provide an abundantly fulfilling lifestyle. But "God will give you abundant life" sounds an awful lot like "God will make you perfect," and that is misleading. Life is not just hard *at times*; it is consistently disappointing, whether you are a devout atheist or a born-again Baptist. With or without God, nobody's life will ever approach perfection. The Bible promises perfection only in heaven, but we get glimpses of it here on earth. God offers us peace and hope in exchange for our faith; perfection is not in the equation this side of heaven.

Materialism Makes Us Miserable

Materialism is the silent enemy of contentment. The deep and constant need to own everything that we like will completely disable our ability to be happy. Lottery winners are far less likely to be happy after they collect their money, probably because they expect it to solve their problems. We need to learn to enjoy good things without needing to own them. I can enjoy the sleek lines and glossy shine of the gorgeous new Mercedes next to me on the road without feeling the need to own one.

We can combat materialism in small, significant ways. Cancel the catalogs and avoid the mall. Practice enjoying what you already own—and maybe even downsize a bit. Make it a daily habit to count your blessings and enjoy the blessings of others, and teach your children how to do the same.

Everyone's Resources Are Limited

There are only so many waking hours in a week and dollars in a bank account, and only so much stamina within a body. We have to make choices about how to spend our limited resources. It is totally unreasonable to think that we can be great at everything, and excellence and perfection are not the same. If we can get comfortable with the fact that we will be mediocre at many things, we'll be better able to pursue excellence in a select few. We can't have it all, but we can have something great if we learn to prioritize wisely. And finding the perfect balance is not possible, either—more on that later.

Other People Are Imperfect, Too
Expecting perfection from yourself typically transfers to others. Friends, co-workers, and other acquaintances will say and do things every hour of every day that are annoying or rude. Expect that, and catch yourself before you jump on someone's case. Practice the modern proverb: Don't sweat the small stuff. Instead, practice more mercy and less justice. Your ability to be gracious to others will yield better relationships and a happier heart.

Stop Being So Hard On Yourself
Find some areas where you can be mediocre. Allow yourself to leave the house a mess, wear your sweats to the store, and let the dishes pile up so you can enjoy some extra time to do something great. Use that time to have coffee with a close friend or create something beautiful. Say "Not now!" to your task list sometimes. Create some space for yourself and some slack for others. Your family will be better off for it.

We can make the best of what we have been given. For many of us, that means bringing our expectations of ourselves from fantasy to reality. Some of us have higher expectations of ourselves than even God has for us, and we will never find contentment until we get real. So cut yourself some slack.

Define Your Focus
Identify your top priorities in life and be willing to let the rest go. Set your sights on just a few things that you are passionate about and that you have valued for a long time. For me, it is my work and my family. It means that I am

not going to be able to play golf every month, read a novel a week, or hone my guitar skills anytime soon. I have to face facts: I can only do so much. I'm learning to accept mediocrity in the less important areas of my life.

Embrace Imbalance

I've got news for you: balance is a myth. Many of the talking heads in the media preach the need to balance your life. This may be possible for people like Oprah, who are wealthy, childless, and have a staff of personal assistants, but I don't know anyone who is a forty-something middle-class parent or homeowner who can effectively balance all of his or her responsibilities. The real world is too demanding and chaotic for most of us. No day is in full balance, and truthfully, with total balance, you're probably not tackling the most important things hard enough.

The people who accomplish great things are not as well balanced as you would think, so let it go. You can't have it all or do it all, no matter how hard you try. Understand that things will get imbalanced every day. Feel free to lose some sleep to finish a creative project—you can make it up next week. Spend too much on your fiancée and save money later. Some people get so hyperfocused on being responsible and balanced that they don't allow themselves to do anything special.

Embracing imbalance should be a seasonal thing, though. Get comfortable with it for a certain time period for a specific purpose. For me, writing this book created imbalance for several months. I exercised less, stayed up later, and graded papers quicker so I could have time to write. But it has been a creative outlet and given me a sense of individuality, so it has been good for me. I've accomplished one of my life goals.

Embrace Your Real Life

Quit looking out the windows at the things you once had or wish you could have. Instead, embrace what you already have. Look again at your wife and remind yourself of all the things you love about her. Look anew at your child and think of the heartbreaking loss you would feel if you lost her. Take an objective look at your job and your home and remember why you chose them and how it would feel to lose them. Count those blessings when your eyes wander out the windows. Thank God every day. Keep in mind that life is fragile, and learn to appreciate what you have.

Practice Thanksgiving

On a daily basis, we tend to fear, fret, worry, and complain about the 5% of our lives that is not going well at the moment. Flip the script—tally up the 95% that *is* going well, running smoothly, and being taken for granted. Get out some paper and a pencil and start writing as much as you can for ten minutes. Set it aside, and then pick it up later. Keep working on it until you have filled up the paper with a detailed account of your blessings, then put it in a place you'll find later. It will be a joy to review it unexpectedly year after year.

Try the following categories for a thanksgiving analysis:

- Family
- Friendship
- Possessions & Money
- Education & Career
- Physical Blessings
- Spiritual Blessings
- Life Goals Met
- Community Blessings
- Recreation & Hobbies

By taking care of yourself and increasing your thankfulness, you will have a better attitude about your kids, and they will benefit from your example of a healthy lifestyle and a happy heart. It's worth the effort.

FEAR LESS

When I was a kid, my mom drove me all around suburbia to my many athletic practices and games: baseball, swimming, basketball, and so on. She was great about supporting my interests and talents and being there for me, but occasionally, the event would be in a "bad part of town" and she would get more than a little anxious. I never knew exactly what she was afraid of, but I could sense her fear before she ever said a word about it, and when I asked her what was so bad about the area, she could not verbalize exactly what she was afraid of. I always wondered what she thought would happen when we got into "the bad part of town." Would we be carjacked at an intersection? Mugged in the parking lot of the school? Slaughtered in cold blood at the gas station for having the nerve to buy gas? I never got a straight answer about what exactly she was afraid of, but clearly she was afraid of certain parts of town, and she seemed to be doing her best to make my sisters and me feel the same way. Outside the narrow slice of the central corridor of West County St. Louis was the unknown, and it was to be greatly feared. In retrospect, I can see that some of her fear was legitimate (crime-rate maps prove that), but most of her fears were greatly overblown, and they limited our view of the world a great deal.

Every parent has fears and blind spots. Fear is universal, after all. Some fears are rational and healthy; some are not. Columnist Dave Barry famously wrote, "All of us are born with a set of instinctive fears—of falling, of the dark, of lobsters, of falling on lobsters in the dark, or speaking before a Rotary Club, and of the words 'Some Assembly Required.'" While we may not be able to control our fears, we can learn to process them better so they don't control us—and by extension, our children.

What Exactly Are You Afraid Of?

While countless fears are common, such as claustrophobia, arachnophobia, and pteromerhanophobia (flying), three basic fears are the most common: fear of pain and death, fear of rejection, and fear of failure. These are directly related to our deep-seated desires for safety, love, and purpose.

These fears permeate our personal lives and are diffused into our parenting. We transfer them to our children just our parents and grandparents passed their fears down to us. For example, in my family on my mother's side, the fear of losing money is strong, so we all have deeply conservative beliefs about making money, living frugally, buying insurance, and investing safely. We brag about the good deals we get on everything. It is a family tradition rooted in a fear of financial failure. There are plenty of other fears that have been passed down to me, and it is my job to avoid being controlled by them.

In addition to the three primal fears of pain, rejection, and failure, early adolescents have a deep fear of embarrassment. It is a subset of the fear of rejection, and it's based on the assumption that the whole world is paying careful attention to everything they wear, say, do, and think. Every seventh-grader thinks the whole school will see the new zit that just appeared. They cannot fathom that nobody will notice it. Fortunately, by the end of adolescence (the late teens), they being to realize that the world actually pays little to no attention to them, and the fallacy is exposed. Twenty-somethings will lose their teenage egotism—at least, they should—and that major fear of embarrassment should dissolve into a minor one. But never forget that young teens are driven to do anything to avoid embarrassment.

Family Fears

While some fears subside over time, others have a way of resurfacing in new, unexpected places. This is certainly true for first-time parents. The newborn child represents a priceless, totally vulnerable life that must be protected, provided for, and nurtured. This taps right into those ancient fears: pain and death, rejection, and failure. And these fears are doubled by the notion that a parent's sense of success or failure stems directly from his or her perception of the child's success or failure. It's a double whammy. In other words, as a parent, I have both my own set of fears and my children's sets of fears, all of which were probably passed down from my parents.

In their best-selling book, *Freakonomics*, Steven Levitt and Stephen Dubner explore the fears that control parents (and grandparents, teachers, coaches, and so on):

> No one is more susceptible to an expert's fear-mongering than a parent. A parent, after all, is the steward of another creature's life, a creature who in the beginning is more helpless than the newborn of nearly any other species. The problem is that they are often scared of the wrong things. Separating facts from rumors is always hard work, especially for a busy parent. The facts they do manage to glean (from experts and other parents) have been varnished or

exaggerated or otherwise taken out of context to serve an agenda that isn't their own.[1]

Rumors and sensational stories rule the day, making us afraid of letting our kids near everything from tap water to corn syrup. New parents fear that their infants will die in their sleep. Parents of toddlers fear sharp edges on furniture. Parents of preschoolers fear that their children won't know how to read before kindergarten. In fact, there seems to be a new set of fears for every stage of development, many of them introduced by marketers of child-safety products and fueled by the media's fascinating and often terrifying stories.

Reasonable Fears

Some fear is healthy; only adolescents think "NO FEAR!" is a great motto for life. That may make sense in the video-game world where you can hit the reset button at any moment, but it's a ridiculous notion in the real world. A little fear is a very good thing. Reasonable fears motivate us to wear seatbelts, drive within the speed limits, and avoid texting while driving. Reasonable fears motivate us to get an education, get a good job, work hard, spend within a budget, and save for a down payment on a house. Reasonable fears guide us from harm, but irrational fears restrict us from achieving our goals and helping others. They keep us from raising our children to be independent and strong.

What Are the Odds?

Levitt and Dubner point out that many parents will not allow their children to play at a neighbor's house if they know there is a gun in the house, even if it is safely stored, but they will not hesitate to allow their children to play at a house with a backyard pool. However, the statistics show that a child is more than 100 times more likely to die in a swimming accident (1 in 10,000) than by a gun accident (1 in 1,000,000). That's 10,000% more likely! But guns, even when hidden under lock and key, are much scarier than pools, so we find it hard to believe the facts about their risks. The authors cite a variety of other fears that have been blown out of proportion, such as flammable pajamas, deadly passenger airbags, and beef riddled with mad cow disease. The statistics show that these fears are not founded on real data, and that the threat of harm by these scary "killers" is insignificant. And yet we ignore the real dangers all around us. Instead of buying a brand-new Volvo with eighteen airbags, we could take a much simpler, affordable, and efficient action: commit to not using cell phones while driving. Instead of throwing out all our plastic containers because we are afraid of BPA, we could stop consuming so much soda and junk food, stop smoking, and drink a lot less alcohol.

Our job as parents is to act on facts and critical thinking, not on mere emotion. Unfortunately, the most common dangers we face are not scary or imminent. Household chemicals, secondhand smoke, and cell phones in cars are not inherently scary to most of us, yet they cause deaths every day. We are afraid of the wrong things. We worry that our children will be abducted by some stranger at some random time, but in reality, in nearly every way, our kids are much safer than they've ever been. Lenore Skenazy, author of *Free-Range Kids*, writes,

> Researchers have found that the number of kids getting abducted by strangers actually holds very steady over the years. In 2006, that number was 115, and 40% of them were killed. Any kid killed is a horrible tragedy. It makes my stomach plunge to even think about it. But when the numbers are about 50 kids in a country of 300 million, it's also a very random, rare event. It is far more rare, for instance, than dying from a fall off the bed or other furniture.[2]

The Scandinavians seem to understand this much better than Americans. In Finland, it is normal for parents to leave their children in strollers in front of a store while they shop inside. Perhaps that is not the best practice in America, but it's an indication that overprotection is not so much a modern thing as it is an American thing.

While it is certainly noble to protect young children from danger, it is not fair to overprotect them, especially as they get older. We need to protect them just enough, but not too much. That is not to say that teens should be left to raise themselves. After all, they need to be required to wear their seatbelts and not talk on the phone while driving, otherwise they will be in grave danger. But it is not healthy to keep older kids in the safe cocoon of home all the time for fear of a rare peril. Our kids need to learn to be competent and independent people who can not only do but learn to do. Protecting them from every failure disables them in the long run.

Responding to Fear

Fear is not easy to control, but we can certainly respond to it in a mature way. It is natural to fear sharks (thanks to *Jaws*), but it is not fair to keep kids out of the ocean. The odds of a shark attack are 1 in 11.5 million—astronomical odds in favor of safety. The real dangers on the beach are UV rays and riptides. Be afraid of the common dangers and protect your children from them, but let them swim— for the love of life. Skenazy says, "Children deserve a life outside the cage. The overprotected life is stunting and stifling, not to mention boring for all concerned."

I believe that as my children grow up, it is my responsibility to train them to protect themselves from danger and give them an increasing amount of freedom according to their age and development. I try not to be an overprotective parent. Kids should be allowed to make mistakes, to deal with minor injuries sustained while they're having fun, and to handle many of their own troubles on their own. The trick is knowing when to protect them and when to let them be on their own. While it is best to err on the side of caution in the early ages, it is best to err on the side of freedom in the later teen years. As parents of early adolescents, we are right there in the middle, somewhere between high caution and low caution. Use your mind and intuition, and get advice from parents you respect.

So, put the Xbox in the closet, push your son off the couch, and send him out there into the world to explore the creek with his friends, hunt with his grandfather, or ride his bike to the convenience store. He is not going to get abducted, lost, or shot. Train him to be smart, have fun, and wear a helmet when riding his bike. Just don't let fear rule the day. It is more dangerous for kids to sit inside eating junk food and playing video games—even though it's less scary.

Jen Hatmaker writes about her journey from fear to joy in her excellent article "Brave Moms Raise Brave Kids."

> Oh sure, when my kids were babies I lived in total fear, because obviously now that they were living outside my body, the universe was conspiring to kidnap/maim/emotionally injure/murder them. It was just a matter of time. Were it not for my diligent oversight, our neighborhood would undoubtedly be overrun by white vans with dark windows waiting for me to simply turn my back whilst they zipped my kids over to the black market. But then I kept having more babies, and . . . We emerged from several potentially life-ending scenarios unscathed: public restrooms, parks, driving over bridges, eating raw carrots, not-washing-hands-after-pee-pee, and I began to lighten up . . . I don't want my kids safe and comfortable. I want them BRAVE. I don't want to teach them to see danger under every rock, avoiding anything hard or not guaranteed or risky.[3]

We need to parent above and beyond mere protection and provision. A strong parent-child relationship will include training in wisdom, for wisdom will serve our children throughout their lives. We should be discussing what is right, wrong, and in between with our kids. It's about training them to discern on their own how to live life well.

Protection and provision are good things to provide our children, but we can provide so much more. Dr. Perri Klass says, "Here's the paradox: If we protect our children too absolutely, we actually end up exposing them to other risks. And leave them without the skills, experiences, and minor life lessons that they'll need to handle the big challenges as they grow up."[4] For example, an infant must be fed, clothed, changed, transported, and even cajoled into sleep, or else he will get sick and die. Now flash forward eighteen years, and that same human, now full-grown, had better not be helpless or needy, or else something very wrong has taken place in the meantime. In order to have success in his adult life, that eighteen-year-old should be a strong, self-sufficient young man who is able to learn on his own at school, have a variety of healthy relationships, and do the jobs required of him. After all, he is a legal adult with full rights and privileges: working, paying taxes, continuing education, voting, getting married, having children, and even fighting in a war. He should be ready to fly on his own—maybe not soar yet, but well enough to survive. In time, he can learn to thrive.

Independence is the Goal

Many parents do a terrific job of protecting and providing for their children, but they are going overboard with it. In other words, they protect too much and provide too much, and this backfires. It disables kids from growing up with an independent spirit and competent life skills.

In a recent article about helicopter parenting, Jennifer Gish gives us a glimpse of the problem from the eyes of a college professor:

Kathleen Crowley, a professor of psychology, says parents' eagerness to over-direct their children's lives has led to young adults who are less independent and creative than the generation before. Twenty years ago, Crowley announced an upcoming test in her college classes and that was the end of the discussion. Now, she says she's expected to provide students with a study guide so they know exactly how to prepare, and she's had these same young adults come to her in tears because they'd earned their first B and didn't know how to cope. Because of this "extended adolescence," when these students graduate and enter their careers, they're now offered workplace mentoring and on-the-job training just to ensure their success.[5]

In *The Price of Privilege,* her landmark book about the effects of modern American affluence on parenting, Dr. Madeline Levine writes,

> Parents who persistently fall on the side of intervening for their child, as opposed to supporting their child's attempts to problem-solve, interfere with the most important task of childhood and adolescence: the development of self. Autonomy, what we commonly call independence, along with competence and interpersonal relationships, are inborn human needs. Their development is central to psychological health.[6]

So why are so many eighteen- to twenty-eight-year-old men and women still in adolescence? Why are so many of them having nervous breakdowns? Why are so many of them socially and emotionally crippled in the adult world? The answers may be simple, but the solution is complex. The parents, teachers, and coaches of those young people may have done a fine job of protecting and providing for them, but they did not prepare them for adulthood.

So how does one prepare children to succeed on their own?

You teach them.

Be a Role Model

Teachers, coaches, and youth-group leaders can be very influential, but ultimately, parents have the greatest influence on children. For better or worse, it's parents who need to be the resilient, problem-solving role models who show kids how to handle challenges without panicking. They need to openly discuss risk management with kids, teaching them that some dangers are worth the risk. Parents don't need to be perfect, but they do need to show their kids the way to live as best they can and discuss it along the way (Deuteronomy 6:7).

Kids need to witness their parents doing hard things, persevering, and being resilient. They can handle and can learn a lot from some transparency. My wife is great at this. She talks to our children as intelligent young people; ever since our oldest son could understand language, she talked with him in a way that most people assumed was too advanced. She did not engage in baby talk after babyhood. They had full-on conversations. I laughed sometimes at the way she explained how and why everything worked to him, because it seemed silly at times, but sure enough, she was right. The kid quickly rose to meet her level of language and cognition. She does the same now with our daughter, who is physically and mentally disabled. She assumes too much, perhaps, but she is absolutely right to raise the bar higher than seems reasonable. And sure enough, our daughter's language comprehension is far beyond what it should be. The point is that our kids are much smarter than we give them credit for. If we teach them every day about everything that crosses their paths, they will grow up smart and wise.

Strengthen Bonds

One of the best axioms of good parenting comes from Josh McDowell, who wrote that "rules without relationship leads to rebellion." In other words, a parent who is too focused on rules and neglects to build a relationship with his child will probably end up with a child who rebels against both the rules and his relationship with his parent. The parent means well but is using the wrong means. Certainly, we want to avoid being an angry, legalistic drill sergeant, and we want to avoid being a spoiling, coddling enabler. Avoiding the extremes is essential. You can set all the right boundaries according to child-development experts, but it's all for naught if you lose your relationship with your child. It is essential that through it all, your children know that you are not the enemy; you are the parent, and you love them no matter what. The relationship between parent and child is the foundation of love upon which everything is built, and the rules you set are the walls of protection. Both are essential.

The key to a relationship built on the right things is to give authentic praise for behaviors rooted in positive character traits. Use praise when a child does something that requires character, not just talent or beauty. Avoid saying "you are so talented" or "you are so pretty" very often. Those are fine compliments, but it's better to focus on traits the child has some control over, such as effort, creativity, kindness, loyalty, self-control, and empathy. Try to say things like "I love the way you get along with your teammates so well" or "I'm proud of the way you had self-control and a positive attitude during that frustrating game." Instead of saying "you are so intelligent," emphasize the amount of hard work and perseverance it took to get that A in algebra. If you praise character traits over God-given gifts, the child will know that you are watching, you care, and you are looking at the inside as well as the outside. Even compliments on beauty can be spun in a better way; instead of "you are so beautiful," say "I love the way you put outfits together and the way you do your hair. You are beautiful inside and out." That way, you are recognizing her personal style and hard work, not just her DNA.

It may seem like semantics, but it's not—not in the long run. Kids want to be known, and your ability to recognize their actions, attitudes, and personalities will pay big relational dividends. They need to see that we love them no matter what they do, and our words can prove it to them.

Foster Independence

It is relatively easy to protect and provide for kids, isn't it? You just keep them physically safe, give them an abundance of fun things to do, and they grow on up easily. That's the American way.

But the better way is to intentionally prepare kids for independence, and that is a much harder task. As they develop, we should slowly reduce the protection and provision—while increasing the preparation. We need to give them meaningful tasks that help the family, rather than coddle them and make their lives as safe and easy as possible. They need skills and they need confidence.

We can foster our teenagers' strength, self-sufficiency, and wisdom, rather than merely providing for their every need and desire. Perri Klass says, "It's our job to help them learn the lessons—even the slightly painful ones—that will give them the skills, defenses, self-knowledge, and sense of humor to cope with a world that contains risks and is not under parental control."[7]

The best way to teach kids independence is not to leave them alone, but to include them in the work of the family. We need to say, "I love you so much, and I need your help. The family needs your help every day. We need you to work, just like we work. We are all in this together." And while they may balk at the idea of doing laundry or cleaning bathrooms, they need to do something that is necessary and helpful. Chores such as sweeping, mopping, dishes, trash duty, and folding laundry are things that are valuable and worthy of payment. So discuss the chores, a reasonable payment structure (perhaps $8–10 an hour for hard work), and get to work with them. Put on some Elvis or hip-hop or whatever makes the work a little more fun, and get it done together. My son prefers Weird Al Yankovic when he mops, and his dances make us crack up—worst moonwalk ever. Besides learning some life skills, he is gaining confidence and learning how much he is needed and appreciated.

It may take months or years to develop a work ethic in the home, but it's never too late, and there is an excellent book about the topic: Kay Wyma's *Cleaning House: A Mom's 12-month Experiment to Rid Her Home of Youth Entitlement*. Kay writes about changing the culture of her home from one of entitlement to one of empowerment. It can be done, and her book shows many practical ways to get started.

Take a Step
So fear less, parents. While we may not be able to control our fears, we can learn to process them better so they don't control us and our children. We can ask good questions: "What exactly are you afraid of? What are the odds? What are the likely results? What is a reasonable reaction?" Then we can take one brave step forward. Take a step toward raising your kids to be smart and brave, to take reasonable risks to accomplish worthy tasks, to learn valuable skills and make the world a little better of a place. It's not about perfect parenting. It's about making progress.

If you have a conversation about the fears and freak-outs within your family, you might be surprised what you discover. My older sister, who has a thirteen-year-old daughter and a sixteen-year-old son, told me, "I asked Cameron what things I might be fearful of that I have passed down to him. He said, 'You freak out if I'm late or if I lose something. And sometimes you get really angry about things we can't control.' Dangit! I try SO hard to compensate for my fears with those things, especially when I can't find something, because Mom was so crazy about that stuff. Apparently, the kids could see right through it." They went on to talk about how the kids could respectfully help their mom not freak out so much when faced with her fear of losing things or being late. Now, it may not seem like much, but I think this is an extremely valuable conversation. It is a family facing fears, analyzing them, and making plans to work on them. Outstanding! Think of all the stress and strife this could avert in the future. That is how you deal with your fears and not pass them down to your kids. Try it.

PART 2 - GUIDANCE

THE HEART MATTERS MOST

Parenting well has an order of operations. Insides come first. The child must feel connected to his or her mom or dad in a profound way, first and foremost. Then, and only then, the child will think about what the parent is communicating.

Heart-to-Heart Connection

A strong emotional bond between parent and child is the single most important aspect of raising children; the rest is details. I can testify to this from my experience being raised by a single mom. To her great credit, my two sisters and I always knew beyond a shadow of a doubt that she loved us, believed in us, and would always be in our corner, no matter what. She never betrayed us and never gave up, even though we tested her often. She showed us unconditional love, and we still come back to her and her values.

Faithful love is irreplaceable. Unconditional love is the common denominator in every great relationship between an adult and a child, whether it is a parent, teacher, coach, scout leader, youth-group leader, or tutor. If a child thinks you might give up on them, he will probably give up first.

Silk explains that "raising a teenager is like flying a kite on a windy day. Teens are blown around by the culture, by peer pressure, and by hormones, and the string is my connection to my teenager, from my heart to his heart." It is often hard to figure out how to communicate your love, especially when your kids are rude or distant towards you. The bottom line is that you must keep trying. Try something old, something new, something unusual. You might miss with some attempts, but the effort will not be missed, and in time those attempts will bear fruit. Just ask questions, give a compliment, say "I love you," look at old pictures, watch a movie, say "I'm proud of you," play a video game—do anything. Just do something, anything to make a connection.

Remember that rules without relationship leads to rebellion. The relationship between parent and child is the foundation of love, upon which everything else is built. The rules are the boundary walls of protection. Both are essential.

Imagine two families with differing philosophies and practices of parenting. Family A is permissive but loving. They spoil their children, but the house is full of love. Discipline comes and goes, but the love is rock solid. Family B is disciplined, but love is inconsistent. The parents micromanage their children to make sure they appear well. Which one would you want to grow up in?

I would take Family A, even though Family B looks much better on the outside. The problem with Family B is that the love is conditional. Some would argue that conditional love is not love at all, but rather some sort of contract.

Love Them from the Inside Out
We tend to focus on how we can protect our kids—by setting appropriate boundaries, establishing positive

activities, and providing safe environments in which our kids can grow. While those are all important aspects of raising "good kids," they are not enough on their own.

The trouble comes when parents react to symptoms, rather than causes. First Samuel 16:7 says, "The Lord does not look at the things of man. Man looks at the outward appearance, but the Lord looks at the heart." Apparently, God is more interested in our inner life than our outer life; we should, therefore, be concerned primarily with the inner life of our children. Unfortunately, most parents focus primarily on kids' behavior—the outer life. But outward behavior is not isolated from the heart of the child. Behavior is a reflection of inner reality. Where there is chaotic, disruptive behavior, there is a chaotic, disrupted heart. It is not possible to fix outward behavior permanently without dealing with the problems of the heart. There is no formula for fixing problem behaviors in children, but an inside-out approach will be more effective than behavior management.

Boundaries Are Not Enough
Every child should know the meaning of no, because boundaries are absolutely necessary to protect kids from dangerous situations. Through early adolescence, we need to train our kids to protect themselves from more subtle dangers: cheating, lying, gossiping, cyberbullying, and social-media addiction, to name a few. But as time goes by, we should grant them increasingly more freedoms and responsibilities, until they are independent and can handle living alone. Young adults of seventeen and older should not need any boundaries.

But well-meaning parents sometimes hyperfocus on setting just the right boundaries and consequences for problem behaviors, thinking that the rules themselves will fix the child's heart. Unfortunately, it is not nearly enough to have the latest Internet filters and the appropriate rules and consequences in place. It is far more important that problem behaviors are approached from the inside out.

Boundaries are meant to protect kids and to train them to someday be self-disciplined and self-controlled. They are not meant merely to establish who is the alpha dog. It's not all about power, although respect for parental authority is important. It's about preparing them for more responsibility and independence. When I set the boundaries for my son's Xbox game, it was not so I could wield power over him and use it as leverage for future situations ("I'll take away your Xbox if you don't clean up your mess in the kitchen"). No, it was to help him have a healthy experience, avoid addiction, and understand that moderation with video games is healthy and good for him, even when he's off at college someday.

Self-Esteem
It is the job of parents to help children earn self-esteem in positions where they are likely to succeed, given their talents and interests. When my son was eleven, he wanted to us to buy him an electric guitar, but since he hadn't practiced on his acoustic guitar, I wasn't convinced that he was devoted. So I told him that he would have to show me his interest by learning twelve common chords. He worked on it for a few weeks and showed a reasonable amount of talent, even though his rhythm was not very good, so we bought him an electric guitar and an amp for Christmas. He took to it like a duck to water, and within a few months he'd figured out how to make some money, sell his X-Box, and buy a much nicer Fender Stratocaster. When he made that deal, he felt like a pro, because it was his own deal. He earned his skill and his prized guitar with his own labor, and that was more self-esteem than I could have ever given him with words.

Dealing with Kids' Mistakes
Some children grow up believing that all mistakes are personal failures, and they dread making mistakes of any

kind. They eventually suffer from anxiety and depression if they don't learn to deal with and learn from their mistakes.

Mistakes should be seen as opportunities to learn something important. Without them, we are not learning and growing. Author Jon Carroll wrote, "Success is boring. Success is proving that you can do something that you already know you can do. Failure is how we learn. I have been told of an African phrase describing a good cook as 'she who has broken many pots.' If you've spent enough time in the kitchen to have broken a lot of pots, probably you know a fair amount about cooking."[3]

Whether it is a left-handed layup, an algebra problem, or a new technological skill, kids need to be encouraged to do things poorly at first, then a little better each time, until they make real progress. Then encourage them some more. "See! I knew you could do it! You have improved so much! I'm proud of you. Really proud."

Don't Forget the Fun
Kids bond with people who make them smile and laugh. You don't have to be all that funny or crazy, as long as you will share what makes you laugh. If you think something is funny or cool, then in all likelihood, a kid will think so, too. Sharing a laugh is a force multiplier in the war for a child's heart, especially when there is tension between parent and child.

My sister once grounded her son for several days, but instead of neglecting him or shaming him, she took advantage of his presence around the house. They played games, went bowling, and played practical jokes on each other. This may seem like a strange way to punish a child, but punishment is not the goal. Connection and correction are the goals. It worked nicely for the whole family; the fun and laughter cut through the tension and created a stronger bond, which means her son is less likely to make that kind of trouble again.

There are no guarantees that our children will grow up well or that they will not have a tumultuous adolescence, but the inside-out approach is always the better way. Rather than setting up the perfect set of rules, barriers, and consequences, families are better served by spending more time together and building healthier relationships. Children are far less likely to engage in problem behaviors when they feel deeply loved, known, and respected by their parents. Remember, children do not care how much you know until they know how much you care. And once they are connected to you, they will listen and consider your thoughts carefully. They may not obey every piece of advice, but they will not ignore you, because they will innately want to follow your lead.

DISCIPLINE

The goal of parenting is to help children be responsible for their own choices, just as parents are to be responsible for their choices.

—Jeff VanVonderen[1]

Raising children is a messy business. Young teens are exploring life and are bound to mess up daily, and it is entirely normal for them to make mistakes as they feel out the boundaries of the world. Our goal should not be to catch them at every wrong turn and punish them. Our goal should be to catch them doing right things and to offer positive reinforcement, so when the time comes to correct a gross misbehavior or rebuke a disrespectful attitude, we are not guilty of "always coming down on them." The goal of parenting is not to have perfect children, for that pursuit will surely backfire.

Parenting requires both discipline of self and discipline of child. First, we must understand that discipline is not the same as punishment. Punishment works on the outward behavior first and foremost. The hope is that enough punishment for bad behavior will force the child into a pattern of good behavior. Negative reinforcement for negative behavior, positive for positive. Simple, clean, effective. Or is it?

I don't think so. In the long run, punishing is not good parenting, because it is based on power alone. It's like trying to catch flies with a flyswatter: it works, but there is no life left over. Punishment can be delivered without any life or love at all; it's rational, impartial, and free of emotion. Take the criminal court system, for example. The judges, jurors, and jailers do not make the laws; legislators do that. They do not enforce the laws; policemen do that. They punish lawbreakers who have been caught by the law enforcers. The goal of the justice system is to objectively apply punishments to crimes. It has nothing to do with the individual. It is about protecting society with rules and consequences. It is about destroying the will of those who engage in unwanted behavior.

Parents must be far more than legislators, law-enforcement officers, and judges. The best parents, teachers, and coaches understand the difference between punishment and discipline. They choose to build relationships with their kids, rather than merely mete out punishments for bad behavior and rewards for good behavior. Instead, they learn how to discipline firmly and effectively, with a personal touch.

Self-Discipline
The ultimate objective of discipline is to teach self-discipline. After all, what is the use of a young person who behaves only for Mom and Dad? What is the point of eighteen years of good behavior if upon release the young adult goes on to live a self-serving, undisciplined life? The goal is to get kids to see that their choices directly determine their lives and the lives of their family and friends.

The best sort of self-discipline is based on a deep desire to live well. We want our kids to see that their character matters far more than anything else, and that it's determined by how they behave when nobody is watching. This kind of self-control comes from a satisfying, meaningful relationship with a parent who exhibits self-control.

Loving Discipline

Discipline should always be an act of love. It can be tough love—and sometimes it must be very tough—but it should not be a reaction in anger. It may take a very serious, firm tone of voice and careful body language, but it should always be about building up, not tearing down. It is training. It is teaching. It is caring enough to explain why certain behavior is immoral, how it affects others, and why making a change is good for everyone. It is about building up a child with love and truth. Danny Silk's book *Loving Our Kids on Purpose* says, "The parent who is bringing learning to a child is not going to try to control the child, but is skillfully going to invite the child to own and solve his or her own problems."[2]

Discipline deals with the heart. A father whose son is lying about stealing money from his sister has some choices about how to deal with such bad behavior. Option A: He flashes his anger to scare the child, then deals out a punishment that fits the crime. Done and done. Or option B: He sees the problem as a teaching moment and carefully considers how to train the child to want to do what is right. The second option is much more difficult and takes a great deal of thought, patience, courage, and love. It is often messy and time-consuming, but it produces love, joy, and peace in the long run.

For example, my fourteen-year-old son is breaking everything in the house. He is growing like a weed, has tons of energy, and is typically busy either building something, eating something, leaving a mess, or breaking something. It is an awkwardness that most boys his age experience. It is also about being absent-minded, which is also a trait of boys his age and related to the fact that his frontal lobe is not fully developed. To his credit, he is helpful in cleaning things up when we ask him to, but requires direct intervention from us to see a mess, much less work on it. Even he is amazed at what a wrecking ball his body has become. Once, in one hour, he broke a towel rack and got Gorilla Glue on our dining room table, which I had completely refinished the table by hand just three months before. After some deep, cleansing breaths, which I recalled from Lamaze class before the boy was born, I explained to him that if there were such a thing as a rage scale that measured from one to ten, I was a solid nine. But I didn't shout, even though I wanted to. I didn't insult, but I wanted to. Okay, so I insulted him a little bit with my tone of voice, but he was a repeat offender. He had done the same thing before to my wife's desk in the kitchen. And seriously, of all the places in the house to glue together a rocket, he had to use our best table without putting down any newspaper, a towel, or anything to protect the table . . . ugh.

After consulting with my wise wife, I explained to him that he would be working with me for two days to refinish the table. I explained that I did not have two days to give and that hiring a professional would cost several hundreds of dollars. He offered to try to sand the glue off, but I rejected the idea soundly. Then I thought of steel wool. Yes, fine steel wool with a very careful hand just might work. So, after letting him sweat it out for a while, I fixed it, to my great surprise, then showed him how it worked—then charged him thirty dollars for my services, which he paid mostly in crumpled up one-dollar bills.

The towel rod was much simpler. We fixed it together and I attempted to teach him some skills with toggle bolts and drywall. I did not charge him for my services because he hadn't done anything wrong, but I did explain that you should not yank a towel off a rod, since most rods are not firmly attached to the wall. Again, it was all about teaching, training, and correcting, rather than merely punishing.

After all that, we each learned some lessons. I even learned a new furniture-repair skill. Most importantly, my relationship with my son was preserved. It was a close call, but it worked out well in the end. We decided to make a new rule: always, and I mean always, use Gorilla Glue in the garage with newspaper under it.

Keys to Dealing with Conflict

- Keep your cool. Give a little heat, but don't go ballistic. Walk away if you need to.

- Consult your spouse or someone else as soon as possible so you can get over your initial gut reaction.

- Explain the problems without shouting or insulting. Be specific. Lay it all out.

- Explain what needs to be learned. Instead of "What the hell were you thinking?" say "Next time, you need to . . ."

- Have a reasonably painful natural consequence. Don't just get mad. Make them pay with labor or money.

- Make it right. Reconcile. Forgive. Affirm the lessons learned.

Being in control as a parent is very different than being controlling. Being in control is positive. It is firm and purposeful. It is intentional. Being controlling is negative. It is manipulative. It employs cheap tricks like guilt. Madeline Levine explains it this way:

How we exercise control; whether we are "controlling" or "in control," is central both to how our children develop and to the quality of the relationship we have with them . . . There is a world of difference between behavioral controls ("Sorry you did so poorly on the math test. TV is off-limits until you pull that grade up. Do you need some help?") and psychological control ("You're going to be flipping burgers for the rest of your life if you continue to be such a goof-off.").[3]

Don't Focus on Rules

Discipline is effective when you explain, enforce, and reinforce the rules—all while maintaining the love that yields a close relationship. But the focus should not be on the rules as much as the principles behind the rules. The Gospel of Luke explains (specifically in Luke 10:27) that the greatest commandment is love, and love should always be a higher priority than following the rules. Jesus was not a fan of the rule-lovers; in fact, they were his greatest enemies.

The Old Testament, which is known largely for its emphasis on rules, says something profound about relationship in Deuteronomy 6:5–7. Notice the intimate language that describes how parents are to relate to God and their children: "Love the Lord your God will all your heart and with all your soul and with all your might. These words that I command you today shall be on your heart. . . Talk of them when you sit in your house and when you walk by the way . . ." It does not take a theologian to understand that this means that parents should sit with, walk with, and talk with their children about all sorts of things, including the matters of God. While rules and parental discipline are a necessary component of the relationship, children should know that they are loved as is, and that their parent is first their authority and then their friend. Discipline begins and ends with a loving relationship.

Madeline Levine refers to this healthy balance of warmth and strength when she writes that "Warm connection is a good predictor of healthy child development—but it's a much better predictor when paired with appropriate discipline than when paired with either harsh or lax discipline."[4]

The Role of the Child

Many people view children as perfectly innocent models of humanity, worthy of worship, adoration, and appreciation at every turn. Others view the child as an incomplete, often incorrigible pre-human that is in constant need of correction and harnessing. Most people view their children in less extreme ways, and will admit that each child is both angel and devil. He is spectacular, and he is awful, but most of the time he is somewhere in the middle.

It's incredibly important that we listen to young teens and interact with them in a way that both honors their greatness and recognizes their limitations. They are not ready to lead their own lives, but they are ready to interact with their parents about their choices. They should not decide where to go to school, but they should join the discussion in an age-appropriate, respectful way, and follow their parents' lead.

Choices

So many arguments between parents and children arise over choices. Which restaurant will we go to for dinner? When will you do your homework? Can he go to the mall with his friends tonight? Some of those choices are for the parent to make as the benevolent dictator of the family, and others are fine for the child to make. Often, it is a negotiation, and the child often has the greater will.

Before you can give a child a choice, whether it is in the kitchen or in the car, you have to be in control of yourself. You cannot, must not, give children choices or power just because you are sick of hearing them whine and complain. Instead, you have to get yourself into gear and make sure you're not frazzled, fried, or frustrated. That's easy to say, but what do you do when your child is angry and you are losing patience?

You have to downshift. Decelerate the conflict. Consider these wise words from Danny Silk, a man who seems to have mastered the art of resolving conflicts with his teens.

> When your child wants to argue with you, these one-line phrases are your best friend. They are your sanity. They are a way for you to kick your brain into neutral while the other person is trying to drive you into the Crazy Ditch. They help you become sort of like a cloud, something that doesn't react—something that cannot be controlled. *When your kid is throwing a fit, it is absolutely the worst time to have a reasonable conversation with that person. Your child is absolutely emotionally wasted. Your child is not looking for solutions at this time; he or she is looking for victims.* This is a good time to just be a cloud. Say, "I know. I'm sorry." You are telling your child, "I am going to manage me while you struggle with you."[5]

To decelerate an argument, you have to stop lecturing and start giving very short responses to your child's complaining, whining, worrying, and begging. Here are some other key phrases that will decelerate an argument:

- I know.
- I'm sorry.
- Oh, no.
- That's a bummer.
- I don't know.
- Probably so.
- What do you think you can do about it?
- How can I help you fix your problem?

You are not giving in. You are strong, firm, and in control, but you are not fighting. You are trying to defuse the situation and get your thoughts together. You are thinking about how you can give your child some choices that will please both of you. You are searching for win-win situations.

Ideally, you will help them solve their own problems. We can help them most by guiding them to see some of their choices. "We give our children real choices when we show them two ways to get something done and either way is fine with us . . . We can empower them to make good choices by offering two powerful choices."[6]

I am not advocating giving in to all the wishes of children or fixing all their problems. Absolutely not! But we should listen to their problems and seriously consider how to help them solve their own problems. And we should listen to their wishes and try to give them real choices that are good for them, whichever ones they choose.

Kids need to be heard, to be given choices, and to learn to solve their own problems. Parents, teachers, and coaches need to be in charge and under control if they're going to train kids to grow up well, and not spoiled or neglected. It is not easy, especially when you are on the edge of the crazy ditch, but in the long run, your kids will learn to flourish with real freedom.

How to Negotiate with Children

In a recent panel discussion about parenting on National Public Radio titled "When No Means No," some moms and a family therapist were debating the extent to which parents should negotiate with their children. The panel members agreed that negotiation is a vital life skill and that parents need to teach children how to do it well,[7] but the big question was this: How do you allow children to negotiate with adults without allowing them to become obnoxious little princes and princesses who feel they're entitled to the kingdom?

The power struggle between children and parents has been a primary issue in every household, in every culture, in every era of history. It's natural. How much power should a child have over his or her life? And how much power should a parent exercise on behalf of a child?

As in all things, the extremes get the most attention. The parents who have total authority over their children make the news with their abusive behavior, and the parents who have no authority in their households make the news with their negligence. The children of these extremists invariably suffer from mental and emotional problems. Some work it out in spite of their parents' grave mistakes, but most do not grow up well. Still, most of us do not fall into the extreme cases. The real question for most of us is something like "What do I do with my eight-year-old who questions and begs and tries to negotiate with me all the time?"

Well, let's start with the basics. One of the most important things a parent can teach a child is the word NO. "No means no" is a pretty good motto for the parent of a toddler, and again for the parent of a teenager (who can often act like a toddler). You want to say yes, but you know better, so you put on a strong front and declare, "No, you can't. I'm sorry."

"Why not, Mommy?" says your beautiful child that you love more than life itself. You can feel the tension rising fast. And this is the moment of truth. What do you do? How about something like this:

> "No—because it's not safe, and I love you too much to let you get hurt."

> "No—because you are not quite old enough yet, but later you will get to do it."

"No—because it's not healthy for you, and I want you to be healthy and happy."

"No—because that's not a good use of our money."

"No—because I love you too much to let you make that grave mistake."

Notice that each response has a reason attached to it. It's not an extreme statement. You don't say, "No—because I said so." Or "No, because I'm the dad and you're the child." The truth is that just "No" is better than those two lousy reasons.

Explaining your reasoning to children is the same as teaching reasoning to children. It should not be about getting them to agree with you just so you can avoid their anger. Instead, it is a brief, respectful discussion related to the reasoning behind the decision. It is training a child to think like an adult. It is not an attempt to appease the child. That would be begging for acceptance, which is a terrible way to deal with a child, although it's unfortunately one we see in public a lot.

Sure, the parent can always change his or her mind; that is not a weak compromise; it is just good reasoning. If a child's reasoning is strong, a respectful discussion can bring about a better decision and a lesson on reasoning and judgment. That's proof of a good relationship, as long as the child shows respect for the authority and dignity of the parent.

Negotiation might have its place in a parent-child relationship, but it's a small one. Perhaps the kid wants to have three friends over for a sleepover, and the parents say no. If the child respectfully asks to just have one friend and promises that they will be in bed by ten, then that is the start of a healthy negotiation. The discussion may be lengthy, but in the end, if everyone stays cool and reasons with respect, and if the parent has the authority to make the final decision, then it's all good. Respect is maintained, reasoning is practiced, judgments are weighed, authority is maintained, wisdom prevails, and lessons are learned.

Discipline is tricky. There is no surefire formula for making your kids behave and have a better attitude in five days or less. But if you keep it simple and focus on building a positive relationship, over time you'll guide them toward self-regulation, so don't give up.

RESILIENCE

This is the beginning of sadness, I say to myself,
as I walk through the universe in my sneakers.
It is time to say good-bye to my imaginary friends,
time to turn the first big number.
It seems only yesterday I used to believe
there was nothing under my skin but light.
If you cut me I could shine.
But now when I fall upon the sidewalks of life,
I skin my knees. I bleed.
—from "On Turning Ten" by Billy Collins[1]

Life Isn't Fair

Life is extraordinarily unfair. Sometimes the good guys lose and the bad guys revel in their victory. Sometimes dictators prevail for decades while children starve and saints are martyred. Is this too much for kids to handle? Dare we tell them the truth?

The truth sets kids free. In fact, we do them a great disservice by shielding them from the fact that life is not fair. Somewhere around the age of ten, they need to be taught that "Yes, life is unfair. Sometimes you get the raw end of the deal." That is a fact of everyday life, yet some of them are outraged by every little injustice.

They also need to hear that sometimes you get an unfairly good deal. Sometimes you win when you shouldn't. Sometimes you find a twenty-dollar bill on the street. Sometimes you get a free lunch. Sometimes you get way more than you deserve, yet you don't whine and complain about being unfairly rewarded.

Our kids need to know that they have gifts, talents, and blessings that far surpass those of most kids in the world. They enjoy things that others will never know, for the world is full of poor, disabled, abused, uneducated, and sick children.

Our kids need to experience the truth about the inherent unfairness of life. You win some and you lose some, and no, it is not fair.

Is God Fair?

So if life is unfair, does that mean God is unfair? It seems logical, doesn't it? I have felt this way during the most trying times in my life, but it never fully settled in me that God was entirely to blame. As a Christian, I felt uneasy blaming God for bad things. Eventually, I came to the conclusion that while life is unfair, God is still good.

Philip Yancey wrote in his book *Disappointment With God*, "We tend to think that life should be fair because God is fair. But God is not life. And if I confuse God with the physical reality of life—by expecting constant good health, for example—then I set myself up for a crashing disappointment. . . . The cross of Christ overcame evil, but it did not overcome unfairness in this life."[2] Pastor Todd Wagner of Watermark Church in Dallas says, "God does not promise to give us whatever our heart desires. He promises that He is what our heart desires."

It is the good news of an unfair life: yes, life is hard, but God is good—all the time. Kids deserve to know this because it will help them process injustice better. The sooner they realize this, the better.

Unfairly Blessed

In our house, the word "fair" is a four-letter f-word. My wife and I despise the casual use of it, and we tend to jump on it quickly. The complaint "It's not fair" will get an unwelcome response, such as, "You are right. Not much is fair. What's your point?" Our son knows that he is the beneficiary of life's unfairness in many ways. He can walk and talk and is healthy, unlike his thirteen-year-old little sister. He lives in a nice house and does not want for food, water, clothing, and healthcare, unlike most kids in the world. And even though we don't have nice new cars or a fancy home theater, he has a private-school education and a private soccer club membership, unlike most kids in America. He lives in a home with two parents who love each other. He is blessed in many, many ways.

Most kids in America are blessed beyond their belief, and it is up to parents and teachers to remind them of their blessings. The goal is not guilt but thankfulness. The thought process should go from "life is so unfair" to "I am blessed in so many ways." Both things are true, after all. Life is unfair, but God is still good, and I am blessed in so many ways.

Pain and Sadness

As I walk through the halls of the secondary school where I teach, I see a lot of familiar young faces. Some I know well, but many I do not. All of these kids have stories inside. Some of their stories are silly—full of light-hearted joy from a life yet unblemished by heartache or tragedy. There are broken kids out there. Many of them will mend well and grow up to be good and strong.

I know the boy who struggled with perfectionism and an eating disorder in middle school and is now healthy, athletic, and academically successful. I know the girl whose mother died of cancer when she was ten and whose dad remarried a woman whose spouse also died of cancer; their blended family is an inspiration. I know the story of that girl whose little brother has Down's Syndrome and whose parents are on the brink of divorce; she is serious, smart, and sometimes silly. I only know bits and pieces of their stories, but I can see in their eyes that they know pain. They have depth of character.

In our upper-middle-class suburban private school, there are also plenty of students who have not yet experienced intense pain, sorrow, or disappointment. So far their world has been safe and positive. Unfortunately, it is a cruel irony that the kids who have the tough-luck stories are typically better prepared for life in high school and beyond. Of course, there are plenty of kids who have awful home lives and are deeply depressed and not doing well in school or anywhere. But in my experience, the vast majority of the real all-star kids have suffered in one way or another. Perhaps Mom has survived several bouts with cancer. Perhaps Dad has lost his job and fought through two years of depression. Perhaps it's a best friend who died of leukemia in fifth grade. Whatever the struggle, kids who grow up well learn to deal with serious trouble in a positive, redemptive way.

No parent or teacher would prescribe it, but the truth is that pain is necessary. Suffering is the prerequisite for service, compassion, love, and a host of other first-rate character traits. And yet we all want the easy way. Every one of us would trade suffering for comfort any day.

A friend of mine was recently bemoaning a surprise pregnancy; he and his wife had planned for just two children, and now they're adjusting to the trouble and expense of raising and educating another child. I felt his pain, but in a moment of clarity, I said, "God has his plan, and it's usually a lot harder and better than our plan. We set the bar pretty low for ourselves." Fortunately, he wasn't offended, and he thanked me for speaking so boldly.

Too often, we set the bar even lower for our kids than for ourselves. In many cases we take down the obstacles in their paths, thinking we're doing them a favor, but we're actually preventing them from digging deep and exercising their character. As long as they can skip across the surface, everybody stays happy. But when trauma shakes them to their core in high school or college, they fall apart, because it's so much more than they've ever handled. We're asking them to run a marathon when the farthest they've ever run is a mile.

Pain is Healthy
Dr. Paul Brand, in his brilliant book *The Gift of Pain*, wrote about the need to manage pain, not just avoid it, as we grow up. "Modern parents lavish sympathy every time their son or daughter suffers any slight discomfort. Subliminally or overtly, they convey the message that 'Pain is bad.'"[3]

So, what should we do to help kids? Should we make their lives miserable to toughen them up? No. Should we place artificial trials in their lives to prepare them for the real world? No. Life is tough enough. It will kick them around in time, if we just let it. They will get plenty of practice dealing with trouble if we would just stop rescuing them at every turn. Your daughter will forget her lunch and homework. So be it. Let her deal with it, and then help her communicate her feelings. Listen to her and help her learn. But don't take off from work to run home to get her lunch and homework and deliver it to her locker. Maybe what she really needs is a zero in the grade book and to miss a meal. Then, when her next trial comes and she fails to make the volleyball team, she'll be a little more able to deal with the pain. Again, it is wise to listen to her and help her communicate her feelings. But don't go meddling in her trouble, trying to fix it all up for her. Don't call the coach demanding to know why your daughter was so unfairly assessed. Instead, teach your daughter something greater: she is loved by God, loved by her family, and has talent that will shine in some other area. A loss is followed by a gain. Those are life lessons so valuable that it costs pain and suffering to learn them.

There is great value in pain. Saint Augustine wrote, "Everywhere a greater joy is preceded by a greater suffering." Let your kids experience a greater joy by allowing them to work through some pain. On my blog, www.growingupwell.org, a mom wrote, "Sometimes it is so hard to watch your child fail, but it really is part of learning and growing up. A wise man once said to his son, 'There are no losers, just learners.' Let them make their mistakes while they are in our care so that we can love and support them through it."

Another mom commented about her daughter's recent failure:

> A couple of weeks ago, my daughter was devastated because she didn't get a role in a play. I was hurting for her too, because she is such a sweet girl and doesn't ask for much. She is not academically strong and theater is her one refuge, a place where she shines. During the painful ride to the first rehearsal, I told her, "Though this is painful, you might still find something good in it, if you let the Lord teach you. Try to be happy for those who got the parts they wanted and reach out to all the others, who, like you, might be hurt and disappointed." My little one did it. She went in there and is sticking it out. I believe she will become stronger because of it.

Failure

Columnist Jon Carroll wrote an essay for NPR's "This I Believe" about the importance of failure in child development. He recalls his interaction with his granddaughter on her first day of kindergarten. "I wished her success. I was lying. What I actually wish for her is failure. I believe in the power of failure. Success is boring. Success is proving that you can do something that you already know you can do. Failure is how we learn."[4]

I once heard a speaker named Dan Miller at an education conference tell the audience about how he learned to fly an airplane. Because he was disabled by polio as a teenager, he can only use one arm and he walks with a serious limp. He had to cancel his first flying lesson because he was sick with polio, but becoming a pilot was his childhood dream, so he kept at it.

In his autobiography, he admits,

> Planes require two good hands and two good legs to work the controls, yokes, radio, and rudder pedals. "Airplanes crash," they would say. "You'll kill yourself." "You only have one good arm." "Your legs are too weak." I heard a lot of dream-breaker statements . . . My first lesson was awful! I had to reach across my body for the flaps, throttle, and trim. Every time I'd reach for them, the plane would dip, tip, and do everything but fly straight and level. I went all over the sky. I couldn't fly. My lesson was a total failure. But I could not give up on my dream yet . . . The next try, though still not good, was better. I tell people, **"If it's worth doing, it's worth doing poorly at first."**[5]

Dan eventually got his pilot's license and has enjoyed many years of flying adventures. He also taught himself to play golf with only one arm, and he's good. He scores in the mid 80s regularly and has a hole-in-one to his credit; impressive by any standard.

Anything worth doing well is worth doing poorly at first—that is wisdom for all ages. We need to embrace failure as a friend who is honest enough to tell us that we still need to work harder, listen to others, think more clearly, and gather more information. Failure has something to teach us every time. That's what makes people successful—learning from mistakes and persevering slowly toward the goal.

Dealing with Grief

When young people experience a significant loss, something truly grievous, they rarely know how to handle the pain. In our culture, grief is seen as a temporary weakness. It is something we think we must tolerate quickly, no matter the severity of the loss.

But by avoiding grief, we avoid healing. If we cover up our wounds and do not deal with these very important things, in time we are a mess, and we wonder why. For some, it stunts their personal growth. People who experience loss and do not mourn are stuck in the shallows. They are unwilling to go below the surface of life. They are puddle-jumpers, splashing about in the rain, ignoring the storms in their lives and in the people's lives around them. They bebop from one fun thing to the next without examining the matters of the heart that are disturbing or sorrowful.

In his most famous sermon, the Beatitudes, Jesus said, "Blessed are those who mourn, for they shall be comforted" (Matthew 5:4). While I am not a biblical scholar, I believe it is safe to deduce that those who do not mourn will not be comforted. They will live without deep peace because they are living in the shallows. Simon Tugwell wrote in his book *The Beatitudes* that "There can be no true rejoicing until we have stopped running away from mourning."[6]

The truth is that the process of grief is good for the heart. It is an essential part of what makes us truly human. It deepens our character. It makes us more able to connect deeply with others. It opens us up to God and His healing power. It makes us appreciate the relief that follows the grief. It makes us stronger and yet more loving. By embracing grief, we will grow upward and onward in our faith and will live richer lives. Grief is good for the heart, and the sooner we embrace that, the sooner we will be living well.

When a child suffers the loss of a pet, the betrayal of a friend, or the death of a grandparent, adults need to step in and help them deal with the loss. The world will tell them to get over it too quickly, and we need to help them process it better. There are plenty of resources out there that can help you have a more productive conversation with your child, and if family and friends are not enough to help a child grieve for a few weeks, then professional counseling should be sought.

Resilience
Resilience is the capacity to recover from adversity and return to well-being. Paul Tough, in his book *How Children Succeed*, explains that even kids who grow up in the most difficult situations of poverty, abuse, neglect, and stress can rise up from the ashes. It may not be the norm for kids of adversity, but with help, they can do it. "The teenage years are difficult for almost every child, and for the children growing up in adversity, adolescence can often mark a terrible turning point, the moment when wounds produce bad decisions. But teenagers also have the ability—or at least the potential—to rethink and remake their lives in a way that the younger children do not."[7]

Young teenagers who are supported by family and adults who empower them will face life's challenges with more guts and stamina than those who fly solo. Those who have a strong sense of belonging, hope, and purpose will hold up better in the face of obstacles. Good parenting can transform a child into a happy, healthy, successful young person.

Resilience is not callousness. It is toughness. I think of certain people in my life who exhibit toughness when it is necessary and sweet sensitivity when it is called for. I call it "kind strength." Kids can learn to be strong and kind, but it will not come naturally. Parents must model that dichotomy, and it should be directly taught to their children. I hope my son is kind enough to recognize when a classmate is being bullied and strong enough to help the kid deal with the bully. And if he fails in helping the bullied kid, then I hope he is resilient enough to seek help from an adult and deal with the consequences. It takes confidence, empathy, courage, and inner toughness to be that kind of person. It may take a decade to get to that place, but that is my hope for him.

One day, our children will be on their own. They will live on their own with their own friends, their own responsibilities, their own troubles. Equipping them for independence requires us to guide them, not rescue them, as they handle adversity. We'll have to help them help themselves.

SOCIALIZATION

Kids Need Community

In reference to the devastating ripple effect of the death of one man in his community, John Donne wrote, "No man is an island." Indeed, we are not meant to live alone. We are made for community. By living and working with others, we enjoy many benefits. When we choose to go it alone, whatever the endeavor, we give up countless blessings. Mavericks may make great movie characters, but real loners miss out on true riches, and unfortunately, there are more and more loners in our modern world.

A large social study in 2006 at Duke University illustrated "a sobering picture of an increasingly fragmented America, where intimate social ties—once seen as an integral part of daily life and associated with a host of psychological and civic benefits—are shrinking or nonexistent . . . We're not saying people are completely isolated. They may have 600 friends on Facebook.com and e-mail 25 people a day, but they are not discussing matters that are personally important."[1]

Robert D. Putnam, a professor of public policy at Harvard, wrote the book *Bowling Alone* about the increase of social isolation in the United States. He believes that people must take deliberate steps to join and remain in small communities; otherwise, they will suffer great long-term consequences.[2]

Our kids are growing up in this isolating world, and it is up to us—the adults they rely upon—to teach them how to engage with communities. As usual, we need to begin by being good role models. If you are not involved in a community, then you need to find one to join, and include your children, so they can see you living it out—the good and the bad. The last thing they need is to watch us continually choosing to go it alone. Interdependence is just as importance as independence.

Too many kids are involved in communities in which they take without giving in return. It is no wonder, because too many adults join communities so they can take from them—until they are expected to make a sacrifice, at which point they quit. It happens all the time in churches, schools, and civic clubs of all sorts.

I have a good friend who epitomizes one who lives well in community. As a high school wrestling coach, he creates a community of athletes on his team. He creates community among his various circles of friends, and he creates community for his family, including his extended family. He is involved in the lives of others, and it's not convenient or easy. While this is admirable, what I find extraordinary is his commitment to teaching his children to live in community. His seven-year-old son knows all the wrestlers and their families. He knows the school building, and he knows a lot of the teachers, who give him lots of attention. He is growing up in this community and seeing his dad interact continually with people, and sometimes that includes conflict and compromise, disappointment and triumph, along with about every other human emotion. His son picks up trash at the wrestling meets at school, and people tell him what a good job he is doing. It is not always a fun job, but it is his job, and he has learned from his dad that although there are a lot of unpleasant things you have to do in order to enjoy the benefits of a community, it's worth it.

If we join communities, integrate our kids into them and give them a purpose within them, and let them enjoy the benefits, the kids will grow up more able to relate to a variety of people in a variety of settings. They will learn the social skills that are at once the most important and the least taught skills in this age of isolationism.

Social Development

Social life. Social skills. Social media. "Social" means different things to different people. So what is the goal of "social development" of children? It is a confusing issue for many.

The word "socialize" has a two-pronged definition. Dictionaries list it as both a transitive and an intransitive verb. The intransitive verb is passive; it simply means to mix with others. For example, when we let toddlers socialize with the other kids on the playground, whatever they learn is not directly taught, but is indirectly caught. The transitive verb "to socialize" is active. It means to make someone behave in a way that is acceptable to society. For example, the Boy Scouts require all scouts to wear uniforms, memorize certain pledges, and earn rewards for the knowledge, skills, and accomplishments that are important to the Boys Scouts of America. They directly teach, reteach, and demand a set of behaviors and knowledge of all scouts.

It is important that we regularly and carefully consider the social contexts in which we place our children. Paul Eugene Roy says, "To live in society doesn't mean simply living side by side with others in a more or less close cohesion; it means living through one another and for one another." As parents, we make choices (or we let others choose for us) about what academic, athletic, and artistic institutions our children will be in, and that greatly affects their development.

School

Many people talk about how homeschooled children need to go to school at some point for "socialization." Conversely, many homeschool educators say things like "Have you seen those kids? I don't want my children socialized by kids who are rude, lazy, out of control, and self-centered." Regardless, it is clear that children affect each other in every social context. There are social norms and peer pressure in every group.

Parents must make the choice about which socializations are best for each child at each stage of development. Much of this is determined by the values and beliefs of the parents. For instance, Hassidic Jews will typically send their children to school, synagogue, and youth group where Jewish traditions are taught and practiced. Hassidic parents want their children to be molded in a specific way and to learn the Hassidic way of life, so they choose both active and passive social situations for their children. This is not just the privilege but the prerogative of parents. Ideally, all parents would be able to choose the sort of school that matches the family's values, especially for younger children.

There are always special cases in which a radically different school is required to meet a child's special need. Some kids, regardless of their parents' beliefs, need a highly structured environment that attempts to mold the child into a more disciplined, productive young person. I have a friend who went to military school for two years, and it helped him get his life on track. That same school would have been terrible for me, but schools are not one-size-fits-all. I taught for three years in an alternative high school in Dallas, Texas, and I can attest to the success of that very nontraditional school for the at-risk kids it served.

My sisters and I went to very different high schools: one public, one private and religious, and one private and secular. We were all very different from one another, and as it turned out, the schools we attended fit our unique needs pretty well. One of my children goes to public school and the other goes to the private Christian school where I teach. We love each school and have strong reasons for choosing each one. Sometimes it's necessary to reconsider school choices each year for each child.

Activities

Extracurricular activities are crucial to the healthy development of a child. At our school, we call them co-curricular activities, because we believe they are just as important as the core academic classes. What kids learn in band, chorus, basketball, robotics, AV Club, or student council is often more formative than what they learn in English and Math.

Our son has been on several different sports teams, and in each case, he had to learn to make new friends. In one case, we were traveling across town to join a great little soccer club, but he knew not a soul on the team. I had to coach him about how to integrate himself into the fabric of the team, and it was a great learning experience. After the practices and games, I asked him the names of the players and what he'd learned about the coaches and parents. In addition, his coaches were great about teaching and modeling positive social skills. In a few months, he had learned how to make friends and how to deal with difficult kids. Most importantly, he gained confidence that he could do it again in the next social situation. Experience is the best teacher.

I believe there is a benefit to putting kids in new and different social situations. I also think it is important to regularly reconsider teams and other groups that they're involved in. It may be time to switch to a new youth group or try a new activity. Maybe not, but sometimes those moves can be far more valuable than you think, if there are good reasons to move on. Don't be afraid to try something new.

Role Models

One of the very most important things I can do for my children, aside from being their best role model, is to place them with other adults who will act as role models in ways that I cannot. In fact, it is the main factor that determines which school, sports team, scout troop, or youth group that my children participate in.

More than anything, I want my children to watch and learn from good people. I want them to see exactly what it takes to be great and live well, and there is no better way than to be with someone in person. The band director is a role model for my son, who is learning to love music in a deep way, not just read music. The Sunday school teachers love my daughter and model enthusiasm for God and others in a profound way. The soccer coaches exhibit great sportsmanship in difficult situations and demand it of the boys. The history teacher exudes a love of true stories and gave my son his favorite book with a handwritten personal message inside the front cover. The special-education teachers adore my daughter and exhibit great patience and model appropriate behavior all day with her. Great role models are crucial for every child's social development. They are the living curriculum of the school of life.

Manners

Being in the right school, on the right team, or in the right activity is not enough. Our kids will benefit a great deal from great teachers, coaches, and leaders, but parents owe their kids more than that.

While it used to be limited to young teenage girls, there is an epidemic striking adults now at an alarming rate. It sounds like this: "Um, it's kinda like, well, you know when you just can't really, like, seem to just um say like what um you like want to say? Like, um, do you know what I mean?"

The epidemic is clearly some kind of communication disorder, but it lacks a name. We need a good label. How about Unintelligible Verbal Skills Syndrome? Adult Communication Avoidance? Teenage Verbal Nonsense Disorder? Arrested Social Development might fit best, because it's really all about kids not growing up.

This communication deficiency is a sign of a larger problem: a lack of social skills. It is more than just an inability to make coherent statements with purpose and confidence. It is indicative of a larger problem, of young adults not growing up in their speech, in their manners, or in other social skills. It is seen in adults who talk and act like teenagers.

Historically, parents have taught young children to shake hands with adults, look them in the eye, and say something positive, such as "It's nice to meet you."

Now, elementary school teachers are tasked with teaching children to say "please" and "thank you" and to begin sentences with "May I . . ." They expect kids to show respect, but they often feel like the world is working against them.

Middle school teachers know that kids need to be taught how to make oral presentations in public, so we teach them to stand up straight so they will look confident: *Don't slouch*. To look at the audience as much as possible: *Eye contact is important*. To speak loudly and clearly so everyone can hear them: *Don't mumble*. To smile and speak with enthusiasm: *Bored people are boring*.

High school teachers require students to call them by their formal names in order to create a sense of respect: "Hi, Mr. Callahan," rather than just "Hey."

Many college fraternities teach their freshman pledges to shake hands firmly, make eye contact, introduce themselves, and then immediately introduce whoever they're with by name. And when in doubt, not to be afraid to say, "I'm sorry, would you tell me your name again?"

The military teaches young men and women how to show others respect with body language, words, and all sorts of other good manners. Ironically, our soldiers, who are trained to kill, are often the most polite and respectful people in our society. It's because they have been trained to be polite and respectful, and they are expected to practice their skills in every formal situation.

I recall being a confident high school senior, visiting with my dad and a college admissions officer (who happened to be a former Air Force officer) about whether I might be admitted to that university. After our visit, my father explained to me that my body language had been all wrong. I hadn't looked the man in the eye, I slouched in my chair, and I appeared generally disinterested. Unbeknownst to me, my poor social skills had ruined the interview. Fortunately, I learned a valuable lesson, and my father took the time to teach me how to do it right.

The good news is that kids can learn to be sociable, and the ones that exhibit good manners and social skills will stand out from the crowd. People will take notice and give them praise. These kids will be way ahead of the curve and will enjoy many benefits. They will be given more than their fair share of respect and help from teachers, coaches, and other adults who hold the keys to their future.

We parents and teachers can put an end to Arrested Social Development if we more deliberately train our young people to be socially adept. It will not come naturally to them, and the popular culture will not be of any help. It takes training and modeling from people who care. We can do that. Kids with good manners will stand out as all-stars. It is simply amazing to see how kids with good manners are rewarded for being countercultural.

When a friend of mine needed some help moving into his new home, he said,

> I had two students help me move this summer. I was a little leery when I learned that they were two of the top jocks in their huge public high school, but I was pleasantly surprised that they had better manners than just about any high school kid I'd ever met. I asked them about it, and they said that interacting with adults like their peers just made them look like everybody else. They said they could have gotten a tattoo to be different, the same way as everyone around them, or they could do something really different and simply go through life saying please, thank you, yes, sir and no, ma'am. I was so impressed with them that I paid them double what I'd said I would.

To help kids get this sort of edge on the competition, we have to model good manners, explain why they're helpful, show them how to behave, correct them gently, and recognize them when they get it right. It will pay big dividends for them for the rest of their lives.

SOCIAL LIFE

Most middle school students spend their school days just trying to avoid embarrassment. It is the cornerstone of their social lives. However, in time, the emotionally healthy kids will realize that being liked by everyone is a lousy goal. Instead, they will seek to make a variety of friends in a variety of settings, without worrying about befriending everyone. And they learn that it actually just takes a few good friends in a few key places to have a meaningful social life.

A child's social life depends more on his or her attitude, social goals, and social skills than on which groups he or she is a part of, even though choosing the right groups is important. In other words, it is more important for a kid to learn how to make friends than to sit at the cool table at lunch. It is more important to discern which kids to befriend and which kids to leave alone. Most importantly, it is more important to have a positive attitude and to be yourself with other people. This is the stuff that creates a good social life in due time. A healthy sense of self is essential in order to have healthy relationships. Madeline Levine explains that "The most important task of childhood and adolescence is the development of a sense of self . . . Children go about the business of forging a sense of self by being exposed to, and learning to manage, increasingly complex personal and interpersonal challenges."[1]

Discussing Friends

Perhaps the most important axiom about making friends is that you have to be a friend to make a friend. Unfortunately, young teens tend to be overly critical of others and too tolerant of themselves. Choosing friends wisely requires good judgment of other people's characters based on their words, deeds, and attitudes. Parents do need to help kids develop that sort of discernment, but they should spend more time teaching kids how to be a good friend in the first place.

Young girls, especially, tend to obsess over the behavior of other girls instead of focusing on their own behavior and attitude. But parents can redirect kids to a balanced discussion about who seems worthy of investing in as a friend and what kind of person one needs to be to earn that sort of friendship.

So what makes a good friend? Kids have some innate knowledge of this, but it is still important for them to think about it and vocalize it in conversations with Mom or Dad. So, start with that conversation. Ask, "Can you describe the perfect friend? What is he like?" Then move the dialogue to "Do you think you are that kind of person?" and "Do you think many people see you as that kind of person?" In many cases, children have all sorts of great qualities that others don't know about because they're not putting them out there. After all, having a good quality is not the same as sharing it with others. Your daughter may have a smart sense of humor, but few people know it because she keeps it to herself. So right there is an opportunity for a great discussion about how to interact with others and how to share your self.

How Boys Make Friends

Boys, especially those between ten and fourteen, need to learn how to make good friends in order to grow up to be effective men. It is important to understand that boys make friends differently than girls. They are very different social animals. One of my lifelong friends, Jeff Lawrence, says it this way: "For guys, friendship never happens as spontaneously as we'd like. It takes props, plans, and risks, but the investment leads to a kind of laughter that is only shared by true compañeros."[2]

Boys need to share certain kinds of experiences in order to make friends, and parents need to give them safe opportunities to have fun.

- be physical—wrestle, tackle, flip, chase, bodysurf

- be silly—tell jokes, tease each other, perform skits, play practical jokes

- take risks—compete to win, jump off the high dive, ride a roller coaster

- go on an adventurous journey with a mission— road trip with Dad, bike ride to grocery store, go hunting with Grandpa, explore the woods nearby

- play with stuff—build forts, make a bonfire with Dad, have Nerf wars, battle with foam swords

How Boys Should Treat Girls

Theodore Roosevelt believed that boys had an important responsibility: "A healthy-minded boy should feel hearty contempt for the coward and even more hearty indignation for the boy who bullies girls or small boys, or tortures animals . . ." Strong words from one of the nation's toughest presidents. Roosevelt had no problem strong-arming other leaders, but he believed that a civilized society requires boys to protect girls.

Boys treating girls disrespectfully is nothing new, but today boys are treating girls not as girls, but as lesser boys, and it is causing larger social problems. It can start as boys harassing girls on the playground and can escalate over many years; it may even result in failed marriages and broken homes. Harassment can become abuse, if left unchecked. Call it old-fashioned, but I believe that boys should treat girls better than the guys.

Instead, what we see is boys bullying girls, and the girls learning their own manipulative ways to fight back and against each other. What hatches in elementary school grows fast in middle school and is full-grown in high school—the battle of the sexes.

I believe that boys should treat girls differently and better than they treat each other. They should be friends, but the nature of those friendships must be different than the ones they have with other guys. There needs to be a much higher level of care and respect. The behavior in the locker room should be different than what they display in the company of girls, because there is a difference between boys and girls. The Bible says it this way: "Do not rebuke an older man but encourage him as you would a father, younger men as brothers, older women as mothers, younger women as sisters, in all purity." (1 Timothy 5:1–2). If that is not a compelling enough reason, then consider this little secret: The way for a boy to become popular with the girls is to be respectful, funny, hardworking, and protective. Girls want to respect boys and develop good relationships with them, but most boys don't give them much to work with.

Eventually, boys will date and marry and have children with girls, and all along the way, they need to treat girls with a higher level of concern and gentleness than they do their guy friends. If they do, they will reap the respect and love of the women in their lives for the rest of their years.

Here is how a good man treats women:

- He never says anything negative about a girl's appearance. Ever.

- He never hits girls. Ever.

- He is polite to girls. No cut-downs, no cussing, and no sexual comments.

- He apologizes to girls far more often than he thinks is necessary.

- He encourages and affirms girls.

- He protects girls. He does not allow other boys to be crude around them, to hit them, mock them, or put them down. Boys should take pride in being the protective big brother of the girls, and the girls will love it.

As for the girls, we need to encourage them to stand up to mistreatment from boys. They may feel that they have no recourse, but as a middle school teacher, I can tell you that there are some good options.

- Be cool. Do not give the boys the satisfaction of seeing your seething emotions.

- Speak to an adult to get some advice—a parent, coach, counselor, teacher, administrator, grandparent . . .

- Speak to a friend or a sibling to get advice.

- Tell the boys to knock it off and call them out as bullies. Total honesty in a strong voice can be alarming, and even disarming.

- Get help from a boy who is a close friend that you trust.

- Use a smartphone to record their words and actions. Then show an adult.

Girls should not put up with abuse. Instead, they should feel empowered to get help to stop the teasing and bullying. Sometimes boys need a clear reminder to treat girls as sisters, and it may take disciplinary action. Either way, it needs to be dealt with.

Dating

Just say no to middle school dating. In my experience, there is no benefit and plenty of detriment at this early stage of development. Granted, there are some very mature fourteen-year-olds out there who are right on the cusp of being able to handle a romantic relationship, but even in that very rare situation, I strongly advise kids of this age to develop only platonic friendships with the opposite sex. This may require self-control, patience, and all sorts of other important relational characteristics.

In response to the young teen who thinks this is absolutely puritan and ridiculous, I would say, "In time you will understand, but romance is a beautiful thing for you a little later down the road. Focus on making friends of boys and girls right now and developing your independent self. In a few years, you will be mature enough to open your heart to someone else in a special way, but now is not the time."

The Pitfalls of Comparison

Adolescents are insecure. All of them struggle with who they are. They ask themselves all sorts of questions related to their identity: *Am I athletic and strong enough to start on the football team? Am I good-looking and fashionable enough to hang with the cool girls? Do I have the cool clothes and gear to fit in at school? Do I like the right kind of music, or will people tease me about liking Justin Bieber? Should I stick with my old friends or branch out to make new ones? What makes me special? Am I good enough?*

Even long after high school, we still measure ourselves by how we compare with our peers. Depending on our values, we assess our self-worth based on things like our socioeconomic status (house, neighborhood, cars, vacations, private schools), educational level, beauty, fashion, fitness, career success, and even our volunteer activities. It's human nature. We judge ourselves and each other in every area that we value. If we value athletics, then that is how we compare ourselves to others. If we value fashion, then that is how we compare ourselves with others.

The band Saving Jane wrote a song about the trouble with girls comparing themselves to others:

> Senior class president, she must be heaven sent.
> She was never the last one standing.
> A beautiful debutant, everything that you want.
> Never too harsh or too demanding.
> Maybe I'll admit it, I'm a little bitter.
> Everybody loves her, but I just wanna hit her. I
> don't know why I'm feeling sorry for myself.
> I spend all my time wishing that I was someone else.[3]

We need to learn that any time we compare ourselves or our children to anyone else, we are falling into a trap. There are three possible outcomes when we compare ourselves with someone else:

- ARROGANCE. "I'm better than her. I must be pretty terrific in reality."

  The problem: I put myself too high and others too low.

- JEALOUSY. "I'm not as good as her. I must be really lousy."

  The problem: I put myself too low and others too high.

- CYNICISM. "I'm just like everyone else. I'm nothing special, actually."

The problem: I put myself and others down.

None of these outcomes are helpful. Nothing good comes from comparing ourselves with others. We will get either a little too arrogant, jealous, or full of self-pity, or we'll have another negative thought.

So, what is the antidote? It's an attitude that says to ourselves and others, "I am no better or worse than anybody else." God creates each person with gifts, talents, and disabilities, and tells us that we are all made in His image, which means that we reflect His goodness in our own unique way. We are all equally loved and valued by God.

God will not care where we lived, how famous we were, how beautiful we looked, whether we got divorced or not, or which college we went to. Our inner lives matter most—"the content of our character," in the words of Dr. King. The truth is that we are all given different circumstances, and some of them are more difficult than others. But we all will have pain and suffering, joy and ecstasy.

Life is hard for everybody. For some, the struggle is physical disability. For others, the struggle is psychological, such as anxiety, depression, or addiction. For others, it is strained relationships with family members. For still others, it is the daily stress of living in poverty. There is something wrong in everyone's life.

What makes matters worse is that most people learn to hide their troubles, so there is this illusion that everybody else is fine, when in reality they are not. It's just one more reason not to compare your life with others.

As a parent, we should be careful not to compare one child to another. Every child, especially the young teen, needs to develop a healthy sense of self, and that cannot happen when a parent is constantly comparing him or her to a sibling, a neighbor, or a peer at school. Comparison is a trap. Avoid it.

Socially Developed

Our children, especially when they are in early adolescence, between the ages of ten and fourteen, need parents, teachers, and coaches who will help them deal with their insecurities and deep moments of self-doubt. Our kids need guidance in their social development, and it starts with loving themselves and continues on to loving others.

The English poet Rudyard Kipling ends his poem "If" with an interesting view of how a boy develops socially into a fine young man.

> If you can talk with crowds and keep your virtue,
> Or walk with Kings without losing the common touch,
> if neither foes nor loving friends can hurt you,
> If all men count with you, but none too much;
> If you can fill the unforgiving minute
> With sixty seconds' worth of distance run,
> Yours is the Earth and everything that's in it,
> And what is more—you'll be a Man, my son![4]

Ultimately, most of us just want our kids to enjoy a lifetime of health and happiness with good family and friends. It sounds so simple and easy, but if we think about it, it is neither simple nor easy. Developing effective social skills is a distance run that will certainly require a tremendous amount of love, guidance, and perseverance.

We must keep in mind that growing up well is a process. It is one step at a time, and wisdom comes with age and mistakes. Don't ever give up on trying to help your children make the very best of their social circles. It gets better and better with love and guidance.

CAREER

"If you can dream it, you can do it."

"Just believe in yourself, and you can achieve anything."

"Pursue your dreams, and don't let anyone tell you that you can't do it."

Countless movies, songs, TV shows, and motivational speakers have preached the shining message of "dream-it-be-it" self-realization. Innumerable teachers, coaches, and counselors preach it. So why would any young person ever doubt it? Most believe it until they experience enough reality to conclude that it is actually a big white lie that adults tell to children to boost their self-esteem. It is a message that feels right at the time, but eventually, life reveals that it is just not true.

How many boys feel that if they just believe with a true heart and practice a lot, then one day they will play in the NBA? And how many actually make it? Less than 100 basketball players per year in a nation of over 310,000,000 citizens enter the NBA. How many girls spend endless hours singing, dancing, and mixing music in order to be the next big star? For millions of kids, anything less than stardom is a shattered dream, and they do not have a plan B for their future. It is a fantasy that starts in preschool and continues unabated through high school.

Additionally, many churches and Christian camps are guilty of inflating the truth about the future that awaits children. Church kids constantly hear "I can do all things through Christ who strengthens me" (Philippians 4:13), and they are told that God will bless whatever they choose to do.

But that verse has often been taken out of context and twisted into a feel-good message. The actual message of the passage is all about learning to be content in any circumstance, good or bad. Our kids need less sugarcoated fantasy and more wise guidance toward real-world success, and they need help both defining success and finding the likely path to it.

Abilities

Telling kids that they can do anything they put their minds to does not necessarily help them achieve their best. There is nothing wrong with shooting for the stars. In fact, we must encourage kids to do their very best and use their talents with confidence and hope. And we should encourage them to think big and do hard things. Young men and women should be optimistic and aim high. However, there is something very wrong with putting blind faith in a one-in-a-million probability and pushing all in. After all, can a child flap his arms and fly? What if he has true belief, good coaching, and puts in years of hard work? Can a four-foot-six-inch girl dunk a basketball if she believes and trains hard enough? Of course not.

Can my son play soccer in the Premier League and be the next Christiano Ronaldo? Probably not. Not realistically, but that's okay. He can play in high school, and perhaps that will lead to a spot on a college or professional team, but that involves a whole lot of ifs. More importantly, he can enjoy it for many years and could always become a coach or perhaps work in the office of a professional soccer club later in life. So, he is pursuing soccer with passion and with a sense of hopeful reality, rather than fantasy. He can shoot for the pros, but he needs a solid plan B for the 99% chance that he will not be a pro. Having an alternative plan is essential for any child who wants to pursue a long-shot career in sports or entertainment.

It is essential for kids to believe in their abilities and pursue big dreams. But the difference is that they should focus on their own abilities—not LeBron James's abilities. Not Beyoncé's abilities. Not anyone else's abilities. Instead, kids need to know themselves, and parents need to help them in this regard. Unfortunately, most kids are not capable of doing that on their own, so it is up to the adults around them to offer some specific guidance.

Parents can help kids learn to play to their strengths. They can encourage them to develop their gifts, talents, and interests. They can help them pursue dreams that are based in reality—and backup dreams, just in case something goes wrong on the yellow brick road. If the child is gifted in math and science and enjoys studying them, then she should pursue them with gusto. As time goes on, kids can learn how their abilities match up with others' and explore real-world applications of their talents and interests. But that takes adult guidance.

Our children need more guidance so they do not go off to college without a clue as to what they might do for a career. It takes wise, caring adults to speak into the lives of young people, saying things like, "I think you have a brilliant scientific mind. You could be a terrific engineer or researcher, and you could actually save lives, maybe even thousands of lives! I am not just saying that. I truly believe it because I know you, and I know about how the world works. If you pursue that with everything you have, you will succeed. I'd bet a million bucks on it."

With that sort of guidance, kids can eventually make real plans for the real world and go forward with confidence, knowing that the odds are in their favor. Furthermore, they will feel that we have their best interests at heart, both now and forever. Studies show that this kind of support is crucial to the growth and overall wellness of teenagers and young adults.

Adult honesty is the antidote to the you-can-be-anything fallacy that most kids believe. Be honest about what you see in your kids, but choose your words carefully. They matter. Talk to your kids about their strengths and weaknesses in a kind, loving way. Be encouraging, but do not lie or mislead them in any way. They will respect your honesty in the long run, and your honesty will uplift them.

Disabilities
Many of our kids have disabilities of one kind or another, and it is absolutely essential to focus on their abilities, rather than hyperfocusing on their inabilities. That's easier said than done, of course, but it is crucial. Our job is to guide them toward success in the areas of their strengths. We should all play to our strengths while working on our weaknesses. So if your child struggles in math but thrives in language arts, do not spend all your resources on getting As in math. Shore up the math skills, but be sure to place equal or greater attention to developing the strength in reading and writing.

Dr. Temple Grandin did not talk until she was three and a half years old, communicating her frustration instead by screaming, peeping, and humming. In 1950, she was diagnosed with autism and her parents were told she should be institutionalized. She tells of "groping her way from the far side of darkness" in her book *Emergence:*

Labeled Autistic, a book that stunned the world, because until its publication, most professionals and parents assumed that a diagnosis of autism was virtually a death sentence when it came to a person's achievement or productivity. But her parents saw that she was gifted and talented, and they guided her to get an education in spite of her limitations. They focused on her strengths.

Dr. Grandin has become a prominent author and speaker on the subject of autism because, as she wrote in her book,

> I have read enough to know that there are still many parents, and yes, professionals too, who believe that "once autistic, always autistic." This dictum has meant sad and sorry lives for many children diagnosed, as I was in early life, as autistic. To these people, it is incomprehensible that the characteristics of autism can be modified and controlled. However, I feel strongly that I am living proof that they can.[1]

Even though she was considered strange in her young school years, she eventually found a mentor who recognized her interests and abilities and guided her towards meaningful work. "I believe that doing practical things can make the world a better place. And one of the features of being autistic is that I'm good at synthesizing lots of information and creating systems out of it."

Dr. Grandin developed her talents into a successful career designing livestock-handling equipment; she is one of very few such designers in the world. She has now designed the facilities in which half the cattle in the United States are handled, has consulted for firms such as Burger King and McDonald's, and now works as a professor of animal science at Colorado State University. She says, "Some people might think if I could snap my fingers I'd choose to be 'normal.' But I wouldn't want to give up my ability to see in beautiful, precise pictures. I believe in them."

The Need for Early Guidance

There are a few kids whose talents and interests match up perfectly with the career they want to pursue from a very early age, but for the vast majority of children, the opposite is true. Career guidance will be of great value to them, as it would have been for me.

By the time I turned twenty, I did not have a clue what I wanted to do with my life after college, nor did I have a clear understanding of the options available to me. I had a lot going for me—a good work ethic, a solid set of academic skills, no disabilities, no addictions, decent social skills, and some athletic and artistic talent. I was going to graduate from a respected university free and clear of debt, thanks to my family. On paper, I had it all. But I was blind. I had no vision for my career. I had enrolled as a journalism major simply because I loved to write and to keep up with current events, but I discovered that reporting was not for me. My parents provided no career guidance. I was on my own. So I went camping.

On a very hot day, I sat on a hot rock overlooking Inks Lake in central Texas and pondered all the things I should have already known. I asked myself which classes and activities I'd always enjoyed and succeeded in. I thought about what I would want to study if I had to go to school for another four years. I considered my marketable skills and made a mental list of which jobs seemed pretty fun. I thought about where I could help people the most.

After an hour of conversing with myself on that hot rock, I was able to talk it out with my camping buddies. Just days before registration for the next semester, I thought of a path to explore: I could get a bachelor's in English, get a teaching certificate for high school, and become a high school English teacher and maybe coach basketball or track. And for the first time in my life, I felt like I had a direction. Fortunately, I was right. I would enjoy that career path. But why did it take an eleventh-hour decision, and why was I out there on my own?

In college, many of my friends were rudderless, like me. However, a fortunate few of them were focused on a single path, and had been on it for a long time. One knew he wanted to be an orthopedic surgeon. One knew he wanted to study information technology and business, so that one day he could run a large nonprofit effectively. Another knew he wanted to be a pastor of a large church. Another wanted to fly corporate jets. They each had a vision of their future, a strong sense of purpose, and a source of everyday motivation. They had an advantage that I envied. They weren't wasting time and money on unnecessary courses. They knew which guest speakers to show up for and could listen with a focused mind. They could sharpen the right skills. And they each succeeded fairly quickly in meeting their goals, and then some.

Wouldn't it have been so much more productive to have envisioned a career path at the age of sixteen, instead of twenty? In retrospect, I can say without a doubt that twenty is too late. Our kids will only benefit from early career guidance if it is an honest running dialogue and is not overly prescriptive. Young children should be given opportunities to explore a wide variety of interests and hobbies. Then, as they grow, parents should help them identify and apply their talents in narrowing fields of study.

Practical Ideas for Career Guidance
- Brainstorm with your child.

- Use the Internet to research what you brainstormed with your child.

- Watch TV shows and documentaries about different occupations.

- Take a tour of a company.

- Shadow a professional for a half day.

- Point out all the occupations in a place and discuss their roles.

- Have your child shadow you at work—more than once.

- Talk about the positives of your work. Explain what you like.

- Discuss a dream job and all the supporting jobs that surround it.

- Start a small business doing yard work, cleaning windows, shoveling snow, babysitting . . .

- Discuss wrong reasons to pursue a career.

Start a conversation to get things moving, but don't go too far too fast. The tendency of adults is to have a fast, furious discussion that settles the issue quickly, but this is not a task to be checked off a to-do list. That would be a mistake. The child may either pick something too quickly without adequate reflection and guidance or feel intimidated and overwhelmed.

Go ahead and start talking with your kids at an early age, but take it easy. View it as a two-year conversation. Ideally, it would start at twelve and make progress by fourteen, but completing the two-year discussion any time before college is adequate. I'm committed to making sure my son knows exactly what he will major in and roughly what he wants to do as a career before he steps foot on a college campus as a freshman. I do not plan on making a college payment until he has a major that fits his talents and interests and will lead down a realistic career path for him. If that means that he takes a semester off after high school to figure it out, so be it. But I want it settled years ahead of high school graduation, so we are exploring options and having discussions now, when he is fourteen.

The goal is not to push your child to be an overachieving, ambitious little adult. It is not about manipulating your child into doing what you want him or her to do. Far from it. The goals should be to know your children and help them find purpose and direction. A good career fit will help them grow up well and enjoy a satisfying and successful life.

EDUCATION

John Adams, a founding statesman of the American Revolution and eventual president of the United States, wrote a letter to his wife, Abigail, about the education of their children:

> The virtues and powers to which men may be trained, by early education and constant discipline, are truly sublime and astonishing. It should be your care, therefore, and mine, to elevate the minds of our children and exalt their courage; to accelerate and animate their industry and activity; to excite in them an habitual contempt of meanness, abhorrence of injustice and inhumanity, and an ambition to excel in every capacity, faculty, and virtue.[1]

John and Abigail Adams revered education as their primary parental responsibility. They did not regard it as a product to be purchased from a respected merchant. They did not view it as a mere steppingstone to wealth, health, and comfort. Instead, they believed that educating their children was their own sacred responsibility. It is no coincidence that their son followed in his father's footsteps to become the president of the United States. May we view school in the same way: not as a product, but as a process that involves the whole family in acquiring new knowledge and skills to experience a deep, rich personal life and to make the world a better place.

Parents as Teachers

Like it or not, parents are the primary educators of their children. No matter how good a school teacher may be, his or her influence will always be second to that of a parent, for better or for worse. Parents teach. We can't help it. At best, we teach our kids more than knowledge, more than wisdom. We teach them to love learning.

One of the keys to fostering a child's love of learning is simply to listen to them, and we can do this well at any time and place. If we take an attitude that says, "I am interested in what you are thinking about. Tell me what is on your mind: the questions you have, the things you are trying to figure out. Anything, really," the kids will know you want them to share what is inside.

Parents can find opportunities to listen to and share with their kids in all sorts of ways: in the car, at dinner, at a ball game, at the mall, or waiting for a movie to start. When we show interest in their developing opinions and their mental gymnastics, we affirm them deep down and courage their intellectual growth and independence. Listening is the key—we do not have to agree with the viewpoints being expressed. The goal is to "model thoughtfulness."[2]

School

Fortunately, education is not a solo task. In fact, it is best conducted as a community effort. Kids learn best in community and with a variety of good teachers. So whether you homeschool or send your children to a public, private, or religious school, you must accept that you are the leader of your child's education. You are the point guard, and you have teammates and coaches who want to help. Seek out advice from other teachers. Ask them for their tips for success at back-to-school night, parent-teacher conferences, and via e-mail. Teachers will offer the best customized advice for success in their classes. Just ask for it.

As a middle school educator and a parent of two middle school students, allow me to offer my Top Twenty List. It is not a comprehensive checklist of things you must do to succeed, because there is no formula, no checklist for success in school, but there are best practices. With many children with special needs, including my own daughter, this list is woefully inadequate. Nevertheless, I am confident that there is at least one thing in here for everyone. So, let's get practical.

20 Tips That Will Help Your Child Succeed in School

1. Know your school options. Whether it is public, private, or homeschool, match each child to the best school situation and reevaluate it each year. Research your local schools carefully: talk with parents and teachers, volunteer, give gifts— anything to be supportive and involved. And do not be afraid to try a new schooling option, which might even require moving to a new district.

2. Communicate with teachers to establish a relationship. Remember, ABC: Always Be Cordial. Treat teachers as you would your lawyer or your doctor. Be respectful of their very limited time and the difficulty of their jobs. Encourage them any time you can, and give them a personal thank-you note for the holidays. And by the way, gift cards are always a much better gift than any cookies, candies, or Christmas ornaments.

3. Consider supplementing with other courses. Look into online courses and community-based classes. If your school is weak in math, look into an online

curriculum or an after-school program. If your child wants to learn guitar or chess, check out what is online or offered by the school district. In many cases, these courses are very affordable or even free.

4. Limit extracurricular activities to two nights per week. Do not overschedule your kids! They need downtime every bit as much as they need time for homework, chores, and reading for fun. Help them create space for those informal activities and for some inactivity. Too many kids are struggling in school simply because they have too many extracurricular activities and are not getting enough sleep. They are tired and stressed out all the time, and it is not their fault. It is their parents' fault, plain and simple. Do not be that parent.

5. Create a workspace at home for academic work that is professional and devoid of distractions. Treat it like an office and supply it with all the necessary school supplies, plus pleasant lighting, a comfortable chair, and a timer for keeping track of time on task and breaks from work. Keep all distractions, such as electronic devices, out of sight (cell phones, tablets, TVs, stereos, unnecessary computers, magazines).

6. Set a study time that is best for the child and the family. For some, it is right after school. For others, it is right after dinner. Make blocks of time for work as well as blocks of time for play, TV, and creativity. Be sure that the afternoon or evening includes some physical movement to wake up the brain and energize the body.

7. Discourage multitasking when reading, studying, or writing. Kids think they can handle it, but they cannot. In fact, adults cannot do it well, either.

Effective multitasking is a fallacy, and kids need help learning to focus on one thing at a time. Allow only soft, mellow music, but no headphones. In our ADD world, we need all the help we can get.

8. Sit nearby as they work at home. Be close, but not too close, in order to answer questions without hovering over them. Read or pay bills or whatever, but be willing to show them some tricks of the trade when they are ready for them. Try to be a helper, not a helicopter. Some kids will like it more than others, and some may not need or like it at all. But try it.

9. Choose a good study partner for preparing for tests. That peer needs to be motivated to succeed, not just socialize. With the right partner, both kids can both learn more and enjoy learning more. Some kids are now using FaceTime and Skype to study for tests. Give that a try.

10. Try a tutor for a short period of time, if your child is struggling in a particular area. Just a few sessions may be enough, and that tutor may prove to be an invaluable resource. Sometimes hiring a tutor is not worth it, but sometimes it's an excellent investment. Many parents see it as an educational insurance policy.

11. Celebrate your child's progress. Take your child out to his or her very favorite restaurant at the end of the quarter for getting good grades and behaving well in school. Celebrate their achievements with special treats in the same way that you celebrate the end of the baseball season or a birthday. Each report card is a milestone. Just make sure to communicate that your love is unconditional.

12. Manage time for your child until he or she can manage it on their own. Help your child keep a calendar for homework, test dates, project due dates, athletic events, doctor appointments, and social events. Kids should learn to know exactly what is going on today and the week ahead. Using an electronic device for scheduling is possibly the best choice, since they will likely enjoy it far more than paper.

13. Be organized when school starts, then help your child stay organized. Pay special attention to binders, backpacks, and lockers. The trick of organization is to have a place for everything and to put everything in its place throughout every day.

14. Use the school's online grade book to know what is going on. Randomly or regularly check on your child's success. Do not wait for parent-teacher conferences to look in on their progress. These electronic tools can help you help children succeed, especially if they struggle with organization. And they can help parents of underachieving students know exactly what their children are not doing.

15. Encourage reading for fun. Buy them any book they want. Take them to the library as often as you can. Pay for magazine subscriptions. Encourage them to keep their favorite books in a little personal library in their room. Reward them for reading a really long book. See it as an investment in their education, for it is proven the kids who read will do better in school than kids who don't read.

16. Get your kids to bed early enough to get nine or ten hours of sleep every night. Ten- to fourteen-

year-old kids need more sleep than adults, especially during growth spurts. Make sure all lights and electronic devices are shut down entirely at bedtime (no texting at 3 a.m., ever!). You may need to confiscate devices at night. Sleep deprivation kills academic success and hurts a child's athletic and social success.

17. Treat food and water as a school supply as important as paper, pens, books, and computers. Train your kids to go to school with a breakfast in their stomach or hand, a full water bottle, and a healthy lunch. It is their mental energy source, along with sleep. Save soda and junk food for after-school treats, and ban energy drinks outright.

18. Eat dinner together as a family at least two nights a week, preferably four. At some point in the meal, talk about school. Go for a walk after dinner to aid digestion and get their bodies moving for the evening's homework and the night's sleep. It all works together—social, physical, mental, and even spiritual.

19. Hug your kids as they go off to school. Leave notes in their lunches. Write text messages of encouragement. Do anything you can to show that you care about their well-being. A little affection goes a long way. Just tone it down a bit as they age.

20. Pray that they will have a lifelong love of learning, for this is the ultimate goal of a good education. People who love to learn will learn how to learn.

Perfectionism

After reading a Top Twenty list like that, you may be tempted to ratchet up the academic pressure on your children in a dozen new ways, but proceed with some caution. Make it clear to your children that your love for them is not hanging in the balance. When approval is conditional on performance, then closeness and affection are bound to suffer. So, take it easy on the academic push. Do not expect perfection, and do not harp on every minor error every day. High standards are good, but academic perfectionism is a nasty curse.

One of the new tools that helps parents and teachers communicate more effectively is the real-time online grade book, some form of which nearly every school now uses. It can be a blessing to parents and students, but it can also be used as a blunt weapon by the overzealous parent to bludgeon the child into academic submission.

Internet-based grade book systems are good for kids, generally speaking. They allow student and parents to monitor academic progress with more information and accuracy than ever. The problem is when parents check grades on an hour-by-hour or daily basis. It becomes an abuse of power. Madeline Levine says, "It may keep a kid's nose to the grindstone because she is anxious about her performance, but it certainly does not encourage real love of learning. Parents' anxiety about school performance leads to children who are perfectionists. It is when a parent's love is conditional on achievement that children are at risk for serious emotional problems. Maladaptive perfectionism is highly correlated with depression and suicide."

Be careful to not expect too much, push too hard, and suck all the joy and life out of learning. It happens all the time when parents and teachers demand near-perfect grades on a daily, sometimes hourly basis, and have the tools to keep tabs on the child's progress. Be careful of perfectionism. It is a wolf in sheep's clothing.

Time Management

As preteens enter the hallways of middle school for the first time, they often feel totally overwhelmed by all the teachers, classrooms, schedules, textbooks, new friends, and homework assignments they have to manage. In fact, well into high school, most students struggle with managing their lives, because there is always a limited amount of time, money, and energy. Truth be told, most adults fail to manage their lives well every day. We all have bad days, but for a teenager, the results of mismanaging day after day can be devastating.

Time management is not about fitting in one more thing each day to be more productive. It is not about putting a smartphone in the hands of every sixth grader to maximize their efficiency. No. It is about learning to live well. It is about setting a healthy rhythm for our lives. And ultimately, it is about living according to our own values, not society's values. There are things we can do to help kids manage their time better in order to live more deliberate, healthy lives.

First, explore the concept of priorities. Discuss with your child what a priority is and why it is so valuable. Discuss how our priorities need to reflect our deepest values, and how the way we spend our time should reflect our priorities. Take the time to order your priorities from what you value the most all the way down to what you value the least. Then you can make an informed effort to spend your time accordingly, making sure that your highest values are not neglected on any given day.

Second, examine the way your child actually spends his or her time. Account for all the time spent on different activities and tasks in a particular week. Sit down and plot out each day, half hour by half hour. Count up the average hours of sleep, school, homework, television, exercise, Internet use, eating, chores, and everything. It may reveal some areas well worth congratulating, as well as areas needing improvement, based on how well it all seems to match up with his or her priorities.

Third, by the start of seventh grade, it is going to be important to devise a system for keeping track of dates, appointments, to-do lists, and memos. It might be just a cheap little spiral notebook or a beautiful leather day planner or a slick little cell phone full of apps. Try a few things and go with whatever works. Every middle and high school student needs to use a planner. Schedule every event of the day, including not only tests and dentist appointments, but also outdoor play time, media time, family time, and social time.

Modeling How to Learn

We must remember that we have to model learning for our kids. They must see us learning how to do new things, whether it is how to replace a garbage disposal or how to cook venison. They need to see us learning, making mistakes, and finally getting it right. They need to see us managing life well enough to succeed in something. Be sure to include your kids in your thought processes as you make decisions daily. They need some transparency. If they see you wrestle with your plans and priorities every day, they will be more confident doing it themselves.

As John Adams wrote, "It should be your care, therefore, and mine, to elevate the minds of our children and exalt their courage; to accelerate and animate their industry and activity." The goal of educating our own children is to make forward progress. We should elevate, exalt, accelerate, and animate our children onward and upward. Take a few steps, celebrate the progress, then take some more steps and celebrate again. If something fails, see it as Thomas Edison saw his failures: as new knowledge about how not to do something. In other words, it is all about learning and becoming better than we once were.

ATHLETICS

Kids love their sports, and so do their parents. The difference between 20th- and 21st-century youth sports is that there are fewer choices now for the casual, part-time athlete. Competitive youth sports is now an all-or-nothing activity by middle school. Many young kids are out at practices or games nearly every night of the week all year long, and some young athletes play on as many as six or seven different teams in one calendar year. Many parents are at every game screaming out their every thought from the sidelines, and coaches and referees are under fire like never before. Our sports-crazed culture starts when kids are very young and builds up fast and furious through high school.

The competitive spirit can get to even the most concerned, loving parents, spurring them to care too much about the team's performance and the games' outcomes. "We are overly concerned about the bottom line with how our children do rather than who they are. We pour time, attention, and money into insuring their performance, consistently making it to their soccer game while inconsistently making it to the dinner table."[1] We can become myopic, seeing the tree but not the forest. For some perspective, let's consider to what end we play.

Most kids dream of playing professional sports, but only about 1 in 10,000 will gain any considerable fame or fortune playing ball. It is a fantasy for all but a very, very few kids who are extraordinarily talented, extremely hardworking, and exceedingly fortunate to avoid injuries and be seen by the right people at the right time. Even playing ball in college is a long shot, especially if a full-ride scholarship is the goal. Unfortunately, the unintended consequence of a sold-out pursuit of athletic success is a young person who is ultracompetitive, overscheduled, and hyperstressed. Burnout is common. Injuries can be severe. Resentment and depression often loom just ahead for the many who fall short of their goals.

I may seem like a curmudgeon shouting, "When I was a kid we would play stickball in the street, and everybody just had fun. We didn't need uniforms or leagues . . ." However, I grew up playing a lot of organized sports, and I love what playing youth sports can do for kids and their families. It can be delightful, and the lessons learned can be invaluable. Youth sports, at their best, can instill noble character traits that are extremely useful at school, in relationships, and in careers. But like most good things, they must be taken in moderation, balanced with other good things.

Unfortunately, it is a real challenge to find a team with a coach that strikes a healthy balance of skill development, competitive play, and sportsmanship without taking up four nights a week and half of Saturday. There seem to be two extremes: the noncompetitive YMCA recreational league and the hypercompetitive select clubs. Choosing the latter can lead kids to push aside some of the more important aspects of growing up.

Those who are trying to figure out a healthy balance to the constant pull of athletics will appreciate Stephen Durant's advice. He is an expert in youth sports culture, and his book *Whose Game Is It, Anyway?* has some excellent advice for parents and coaches of young athletes. He focuses on three main points: character development, skill development, and age-appropriate expectations. All three priorities are in contrast with what he calls the "scoreboard outcomes."

These wise words ring true, but we must check our attitudes at every practice, every game, and every related conversation. Whose game is it, anyway? And why exactly are we playing?

Middle school is the time and place to work with kids on being coachable and gaining a strong work ethic. It's the training ground for learning how to handle loss, jealousy, pride, embarrassment, and a host of other awkward issues—before high school, when the kids are playing in front of crowds of their peers. Play ball, have fun, work hard, study well, be a good team player, and see where it leads.

Role Models
Character is built slowly and surely, sometimes in humble places, until one day it shines enough to inspire another person to become better than they once were. Learning to win and lose with a gracious, positive attitude is a sign of good character. There are role models all around us—at home, at church, driving the bus, coaching another game, changing diapers, disciplining the toddlers, cleaning the house, teaching new lessons, telling the stories, cracking jokes, bandaging the wounded, and loving the unlovely.

There are hundreds of little league and high school coaches in every community who spend hours each week planning and leading practices, making phone calls, devising strategies, and inspiring kids to give their very best when they are tired and frustrated. They encourage kids to be good, play hard, and learn from their mistakes. And they get paid little or nothing for it. Let's make sure our kids appreciate them for what they do—and make sure they get their athletic role models locally, instead of from ESPN.

My experience as a young athlete was terrific. I enjoyed a lot of success on highly competitive teams, and I had some admiration from my peers, which built up my self-esteem at a young age. I enjoyed and learned from plenty of thrilling and heartrending experiences on the football field, basketball court, and track. But for all the excitement and accolades, I gained the most from being around coaches and parents who were good role models. My mom taught me to recognize the bad traits of some coaches and to learn from their bad behavior. But a handful of coaches, including Coach Miller, Coach Chancey, Coach Small, and Coach Macintosh, instructed me, encouraged me, and corrected me in significant ways. They showed me how to be a man, not just a boy, in mostly unspoken ways. Just by being in their presence so much, I absorbed some of their characteristics; that is what I love most about sports.

Back in the 1980s, I badly needed some positive role models, and as I look around at youth culture now, I see that now, more than ever, our kids need good role models to show them—not just tell them—how to grow up well.

Parental Guidance in Sports

There is not much you can do about the fact that kids—boys, especially—will judge each other first on athleticism. But you can train kids to see through that thin veneer and to learn the value of all those other skills and qualities that they will need in the last sixty years of their lives.

Parents have the ability to speak into kids' lives and cut through the lies and the nonsense of the culture. Here are some thoughts on teaching kids to swim in the deep end of life:

1. Use the power of words. Kids need to hear so much more than "Great game, Jack!" or "You are such a pretty girl, and so athletic, too." Instead, praise them for their creative problem-solving on the team or the way they encourage their teammates. Praise them for the gutsy way they deal with being sick and making up all their schoolwork on time. Praise their character when it is good, and correct it when it is bad. Your words must reinforce your values: you prove what is important with what you say and do.

2. Point out role models. Talk about which players exhibit the best characteristics. Point out real people who are impressive, not just celebrities— although it also helps to point out the famous people who exemplify good character. Root for the good guys.

3. Give kids opportunities to do new things that stretch them. Do not let them get too comfortable. Examine how they spend their free time, and make sure that it is diversified among a variety of activities throughout the year and involve varying social situations (art, music, service, scouts, sports, etc.). Just be careful not to overschedule them. Schedule in some downtime each week.

4. Show and tell them about your world. Kids need to get glimpses of what they will be doing later in life. Use the dinner table as the place to introduce them to the larger world; do not let them just get it from TV. Take them to work once a year. Talk about what your friends are accomplishing in their

careers. Kids can learn to understand and eventually appreciate those things.

5. Keep their eyes on the road ahead. Make sure that they see that life is a long journey and that youth is the best time to try new things and learn what they can and cannot do well. Help them learn who God has made them to be, and guide them in the way that you think will maximize their long-term success and significance.

The bottom line is that kids need to develop a wide base of skills and characteristics. They must not be allowed to lean too heavily on the crutches of athletic talent, because those crutches only last so long. Quarterbacks and cheerleaders make great prom kings and queens, but that success is not going to translate to the real world unless those kids grow up in other ways. Throwing a fifty-yard spiral won't help you much after you are twenty. It is better to diversify a little and have a backup plan or two. Well-rounded kids can handle what life throws at them long after their athleticism becomes irrelevant. Left on their own, kids will not grow up well, but with adult care and guidance, they can be well prepared for a truly significant and rewarding life throughout and well beyond those "glory years" in school.

Overscheduling

We live in a society that says we can always do more, own more, and be more of everything. Much of that is good. We are a can-do society, and that drives us onward and upward in many ways. However, there are some negative consequences to this drive for more, more, more, and many young people, even as young as seven years old, are too busy. They have school, church, organized sports, music lessons, and homework. They are too busy to play, create, and be outdoors. In most cases, if not all, it's a trickle-down effect; too-busy parents make kids too busy.

But overcommitment is to the soul what monthly payments are to the budget. We are writing checks over time that our body, mind, and soul cannot pay for in full. When we set kids up with too many good activities, they get stressed and exhausted and they end up doing a whole lot of things pretty poorly. Instead of programming our kids to live this way at a very impressionable age, we need to deliberately limit our obligations; otherwise, they may never get out of that rut. never get out of that rut.

Learning by Losing

NFL Hall of Fame coach Vince Lombardi famously quipped, "Winning isn't everything, it's the only thing." This defines the modern American's view of sports. The Olympic runner who crosses the finish line just behind the winner is the first one to lose. The announcers will expound upon all the things he did wrong to lose the race, but in reality, he is the second fastest runner in the world! He should be applauded for his training and for his Herculean effort in the race, but instead he is pitied for losing. Our culture praises the winner and either pities or scolds the rest.

After a weekend out of town at my son's soccer tournament, I grew tired of hearing "Did you win?" It was, hands down, the single most popular question of the weekend. Even strangers in the hotel would ask my uniformed son, "Didja win?"

And each time we would sadly reply, "No," which would be followed by an awkward silence. For an eleven-year-old boy who loves to win, it is not easy to lose all three games. Especially when you drive five hours each way to make it happen.

Zero for three. Winless. Losers. And yet he and his teammates played so hard and so well—they did all that their coach asked them to do. They pressured the ball on defense. They stayed spread out. They passed the ball much better than all the other teams. They put together better plays and took more shots than the other teams. They kept playing hard, giving their best—body, mind, and heart—even when they were knocked down over and over without a foul being called. Shot after shot would hit the goalposts or just miss the net. But in each game, they would give up a cheap breakaway goal to the other team. It was frustrating, because we should have won at least one of those games, if not all three.

My wife and I had several talks over the weekend about how frustrating it was to lose those well-played, well-fought games. At first, we were mad and sad, but ultimately we realized that we were all wrong. We needed to see the bigger picture. This was a test of our belief that winning and losing are not all-important.

We recalled that our coach, and our soccer club as a whole, wanted to "play the game for the game's sake." And at that age level, their stated goals were "smartness of play; overall field vision; desire for the next step." They were all about loving the game, playing it the right way, and helping the kids become better players.

Does that mean that winning was not the ultimate goal? Nope, it was about fourth on the list. Yet that feels very un-American. Maybe that is why Americans don't like soccer; there is not a lot of scoring, and individual stars don't stand out much. And quite often, the better team walks away with a tie or a loss.

Our five-hour trip back home from that tournament was full of discussions about how our son has improved and how he needs to improve. We talked about how life is like soccer: it takes teamwork, hard work, and smart work. Winning will come eventually, but it can be a lot of fun along the way if you have the right perspective, win or lose.

It is always good to talk about the amount of effort given and the choices made during the game. "How do you think you played?" is a good discussion starter. Remember to focus on effort, character, and the love of the game, rather than scoreboard outcomes.

LOOKING GOOD

Everybody knows who she is. All the kids stare at her, trying to figure out what makes her so pretty. What's her secret? She is naturally photogenic, with symmetrical features, high cheekbones, clear skin, straight white teeth, and bright eyes. Her hair easily folds into the latest hairstyle, and her figure just gets better each year. She is a young Venus, goddess of love and beauty. She simply smiles politely and everybody adores her. She does not have to speak intelligently, get good grades, or have a snappy sense of humor. Her name is written on other kids' binders at school and all eyes are on her in the halls. While many are jealous of her, most girls want to be her. She can be boring or rude, and yet boys still want to be around her.

It is not fair, but it is real. It is the economy of the adolescent world, as well as the media, that broker of adolescent imagery. Male athleticism and female beauty are commodities, and it seems like everyone wants to capitalize on them. The boys want chiseled muscles and name-brand athletic wear. The girls want to be cute and a little sexy and to have a complex array of clothing, accessories, makeup, hairstyles, and iPhones. The advertisers and the companies they represent want it exactly that way, because they sell billions of dollars of products each year to our kids, who they've dubbed "tweens."

Businesses see young children as a target market that is not fully explored. They go deeper and deeper into youth culture to find more market share. For example, Victoria Secret used to be a high-end lingerie store for women, but now includes young teens with their "Pink" line of lingerie[1], supposedly intended for fifteen- to twenty-two-year-old girls. Their hope is to not only increase sales, but ultimately to establish a lifetime of brand loyalty in these young girls. That is the greatest prize for a brand marketer; it is one thing to sell an expensive set of pajamas, but it is a grand slam to get a kid to buy a lifetime of underwear and perfume.

Thirteen-year-old boys and girls care a lot about their looks. That is human nature, and in moderation, it is a good thing. But Americans are not known for moderation. We tend to obsess. Young girls obsess over their looks at increasingly younger ages. Ten-year-old girls are buying makeup, designer clothes, and jewelry, to the delight of manufacturers. Young boys are buying expensive shoes, athletic wear, and body sprays in order to seem stronger, more handsome, and more masculine than their age allows.

Actually, it is the parents of these young kids who are spending large amounts of money, so let's not blame the kids. It is the parents who are ultimately responsible.

We live in a celebrity-obsessed culture, and that plays into the marketing machine. Our favorite actors appear in fashion advertisements and on the covers of magazines. They are on all the talk shows, as well. The Internet is happy to deliver a heaping dose of celebrity, beauty, and style on nearly every website. Online ads are customized by marketers and programmers to show each of us exactly the right image that will make us want to buy their products.

Young teens live in the same environment we do, even if we think we are shielding them from society. They see the billboards, the TV ads, the magazine covers, and most of the other imagery that we see, even if they are not watching any R-rated movies. The world outside their home is teaching them things that they are not old enough to fully understand. The cultural messages are unavoidable:

- Beautiful people are just better. They get more respect and privileges.

- Beautiful people are loved. Without beauty, you will be lonely.

- Beauty can be bought with the right products, and the expense will be worth it.

- Beauty and sexuality can be used to get what you want, including Mr. Right.

As a result, many young teens are confused and lose confidence in themselves. Their identity no longer makes much sense. In many cases, early confusion about beauty and sexuality results in low self-esteem, depression, and eating disorders.

Inner Beauty

As a parent, the natural inclination is to shrug off the adolescent obsession with image and hold fast to the notion that kids will outgrow their vanities. But it is not enough to trust that they will be able to separate the truth from the lies on their own. Kids need adults to make sense of the world with them and gain a healthy perspective on their self-image and self-worth.

The biblical approach to beauty is to "Do not let your adorning be external—the braiding of hair and the putting on of gold jewelry, or the clothing you wear— but let your adorning be the hidden person of the heart with the imperishable beauty of a gentle and quiet spirit, which in God's sight is very precious." (1 Peter 3:3–4). Historically, some people have taken this as a commandment to never wear jewelry, fine clothes, or a particular hairstyle, but these legalists are missing the point. The theme of the passage is to focus on the inner life first and foremost: the inner person matters most.

External beauty is elusive, shallow, and fleeting, but inner beauty is obtainable, satisfying, and eternally valuable—it is just not as immediate, apparent, or exciting. Proverbs 31:30 says, "Charm is deceptive and beauty is vain." We should explain this often to our kids. We should not assume that they understand it. Our girls especially need to know this as soon as possible. We can help them see real beauty, but as usual, it is going to take a lot of love, involvement, and direction. And we are going to have to be good role models by handling our own outward images in healthy ways, for our kids will emulate us, for better or for worse.

Practical Advice

Rather than expounding at length about the various causes and peculiarities of our struggles with beauty and youth in 21st-century America, I want to explore possible solutions. And since the problem is so complicated, a silver-bullet prescription like "spend more time with your children" is not sufficient.

I will attempt to offer some age guidelines that are more specific than just ten to fourteen, but ultimately, it is your responsibility to decide what is best for your child and your family.

Security vs. Insecurity

The most important part of helping your child navigate the dangerous waters of self-esteem, self-worth, and body image is conveying that you love them as is. Kids need to know that their parents and other adults love them just the way they are, and that image is not a factor in that love. They must feel secure in their own skin. Every child, no matter the age, needs to be affirmed for who she is inside. And often. Consider some of these useful messages:

- "You are beautiful inside and out." (Say this when they are not dressed up.)

- "I like you just the way you are." (Say this when they aren't doing something special.)

- "God made you special, and He loves you very much." (One of our family's favorites.)

- "I love you." (Always appropriate.)

- "I am proud of you." (More powerful than you would think.)

- "Even though we don't like each other right now, I love you and always will."

Makeup and Hair

Most parents of daughters can attest to lengthy debates, tears, conversations, and raging arguments about hair and makeup. What on earth makes a ten-year-old girl want to wear makeup and color her hair?

The big collision with this tricky issue, as well as concerns about clothes and even boyfriends, is usually in sixth grade. Of course, it can happen much sooner, but the conflicts usually start around twelve years old. I recommend not allowing girls to get involved with any of these things until seventh grade, and after that, it's best to proceed slowly and with caution.

So when your adorable daughter asks if she can buy mascara and straighten her hair, you might return her questions with your own: "Why do you want a new hairstyle and face when you are so beautiful already?" If she says "to be like you," then you have your work cut out for you. Keep asking questions:

- What are some good purposes for makeup?

- What are some bad reasons to wear makeup?

- What is the purpose of a fancy hairstyle or a color change?

- Are you aware of the financial cost and the damage to your hair from coloring?

- How long will it take every day to work on your hair and makeup?

- Do you think it will make you happy? Why or why not?

Beyond that, make sure your daughter understands that the goal of looking attractive should not be to attract boys. Help her think of boys as her friends and brothers. Explain that she does not need to live up to some standard set by the beauty industry, and that your family is not going to spend a lot of money on beauty products. This should be a discussion that focuses on building inner beauty, spiritual depth, and quality relationships. These are things that have lasting value and are not easily acquired. They are developed and earned and yield great respect.

If the conversations are not going so well, then bring Dad, her big brother, or another man into the conversation to reinforce the notion that inner beauty is the most important thing, and it is not something Daddy's credit card can buy. The more voices singing the same tune, the better.

It is crucial that kids enjoy their childhood and not attempt to grow up too fast. My advice is to go slowly, talk it out as you go, and adopt one thing at a time. Keep in mind that some concerns about appearance do require attention early on so kids can avoid humiliation; for instance, acne can be tremendously trying, and a visit to a dermatologist can be very valuable. Having a particularly noticeable scar or hair that is extremely kinky and unmanageable can be traumatizing to a sixth- or seventh-grader, and a consultation with a professional can be a great idea. In some cases, young teens look to hair and makeup for self-defense, not out of vanity. Every child and situation is different, so I encourage lots of honest conversation with every decision.

Clothes

A significant part of a young teen's identity is clothes. Kids will judge, tease, and compliment each other about their clothes, shoes, and accessories, and they will study and shop for the image they want to project. Some of this is good; fashion is a form of art, and it can be a healthy expression of personality and feelings. Clothing can be beautiful and honorable to the human form. It can be fun and bring joy to ourselves and others.

But our culture tends to obsess, and some of our kids' interest in fashion can be unhealthy—a desperate need for attention and an expression of materialism, vanity, or even addiction. Buying trendy clothes for growing kids can put families in a prison of debt. And so much of the clothing in the malls is sexy and encourages young girls to use it to gain attention from boys and discover sexual power at way too early an age. We have to guide our kids carefully—and not turn them loose in the mall with sixty dollars or a credit card, as so many upper-middle-class parents do.

Guiding a child's sense of style is extremely difficult, but families need to establish basic guidelines that still allow certain freedoms. My son, for instance, loves to wear big, soft, floppy bomber hats. I allow this most of the time, even though I hate it. We compromise often about the styles of jeans and t-shirts that he wears, but we choose our battles and don't try to control every bit of his life.

As you shop for clothing with your child, the following questions can encourage good decisions and help avoid knock-down, drag-out arguments:

- What do we need? What is the function of the clothing that we are looking for?

- When do we need this? Is it urgent, or are we just researching today?

- What do you want? What style are you looking for?

- What is our budget? How can we use our money as wisely as possible?

- Where do you intend to wear this? Here is where you will not wear this . . .

Body Image and Weight

Americans are not known for having a healthy relationship with food. We have issues, to say the least; we love our food, but we consume it in extremes, and our kids learn from our bad habits. Obesity is a massive problem, as is anorexia, even among ten- to fourteen-year-olds. Being skinny is an obsession for many girls; being "ripped" is the obsession for many boys. And not enough people are interested in good old-fashioned health.

We adults need to be the voice of reason, the ones who eat in moderation, exercise for health's sake, and are not obsessed with our weight or body image. Easier said than done, sure, but we must realize that the apple does not fall far from the tree. Our kids watch, listen, and learn from us. If we talk about losing pounds and fitting into tight jeans and how we look all the time, then the kids will learn that looks and weight are everything. Instead, we can try to model a healthy, sane approach to food and weight, and our kids will likely follow along.

But action must be paired with the right words. We should always emphasize health as the goal, not beauty or weight. We exercise to reduce stress and become healthier, not for beauty. Do not say to your child, "You look so skinny (or fat) in that outfit." We should not say skinny or fat at all, since those words are loaded in our culture. Instead, we should talk about food as energy and exercise as a stress reducer. And each person in the family will have different metabolisms and issues, so each family member may have different goals. One may be working to build muscle for football with protein-rich foods, while another may be focusing on sugar regulation for a pre-diabetic condition. We all have different diets, according to our age and health needs, but we all are striving for health and wellness, not beauty.

Our words should be encouraging and intended to lift up the body image of a child. We should say things like, "You are a good-lookin' kid, you know that?" Or "You are looking really healthy. You must be taking care of yourself well." Just remember that kids listen very carefully to what you say, and they will take things the wrong way if you aren't careful. Be kind. They will grow up well if you speak light into their lives.

Social Media

An important part of the 21st-century teenager's life is his or her smartphone. These all-in-one devices are more than just communication tools; they are fashion accessories. Even the cases are fashion statements, but even so, 90% of middle school kids' phones have cracked screens. Most kids will tell you that their phone is their most important possession and that they literally could not live without it. Their addiction is severe; most of them will admit it outright. It seems that sixth-grade graduation has become the time when all the kids get cell phones, and it amazes me how many kids have the highest-end devices with unlimited minutes.

Image is everything on smartphone apps, Instagram, and Twitter—the new ways teenagers make themselves known. They take their best and craziest pictures and broadcast them on social networks to their friends and their friends' friends. Unfortunately, a lot of kids are getting themselves and their friends in a lot of trouble by posting images that are in poor taste, and other kids are using those images with even less discretion.

I am not a fan of middle school kids having cell phones, but if your child has a smartphone, please disable the social media capabilities. I will write much more on this later, but believe me when I say that kids hurt each other with social media in ways that you would not believe. Every kid who participates in social media gets hurt by someone, and it is avoidable and unnecessary. For me, this is not a place to compromise.

Vision of Beauty

Wouldn't it be great if our middle school kids had a cool sense of style and personal beauty that was unique from ours and from pop culture but not totally obnoxious? Wouldn't it be great if our kids were more concerned about their physical and mental health than the way they looked? Wouldn't it be great if they had enough self-esteem and self-worth to not feel the need for a boyfriend or girlfriend to validate them?

It is possible to help them become that confident. A strong, positive sense of self in the early teen years may take a while, and there is no formula. It may take a few rough years filled with many conversations and debates, but that's just good parenting. Don't give up.

THE NEW MEDIA

Nobody seems to know what to do about their young kids' involvement with computers, smartphones, and social media. The Internet is full of blog posts and editorials by parents who are completely bewildered by the digital lives of their children. Parents hear horror stories of pedophiles, pornography, sexting, and cyberbullying. But how many parents feel confident that they can help their kids avoid the dark side of the new wave of media and technology? Most of us, if we are totally honest, will admit that we have a lot to learn about navigating new media, rather than just outlawing or allowing it all.

Self-examination is the healthy place to start, before we get into the nuts and bolts of technology. Parental attitudes and abilities range a great deal. See if you can identify where you stand right now: hands off, hands tied, hands open, or hands full?

Hands Off
Some parents do not want to know what is going on with their kids and their new-fangled media, because the whole thing freaks them out and they feel paralyzed. For them,

ignorance is bliss. They do not want to know more, so they ignore the whole thing. They are scared and worried that they will just make things worse by getting involved. Their attitude is that if the kids are quiet with their devices, then all is well. It is in their interest to not know what is going on.

Hands Off = unwilling and unmotivated to learn and help

Hands Tied

Other parents have a pretty good idea about what is going on with their kids online, but they feel helpless. They understand the technology pretty well; after all, they use it themselves. They may have seen exactly what their kids are doing online, and they may not be happy about it. The problem is not ignorance, but they do not want to invade their children's privacy or upset them by treading into shark-infested waters by limiting their children's use of technology. To them, the problem is enforcement. They cannot imagine the wrath of their kids if they intervene, so their hands are tied.

Hands Tied = informed, but unwilling to learn and help

Hands Open

These parents want to protect their kids and are willing to learn, but they do not have a clue how. They mean well, and they are willing to work at it, but they just do not understand the technology and its inherent problems. These parents are begging for information, advice, and opportunities to help their kids. These parents are ready to learn and to help.

Hands Open = uninformed, but willing to learn and help

Hands Full

These parents are working to understand the new media and technology. They talk with their friends, teachers, and youth-group workers, and research online to try to keep up with the digital world their kids are dealing with. They may attend a workshop or subscribe to a newsletter on media literacy. They talk with their kids about what they are doing online, what they like to watch and listen to, and how to navigate new media safely and effectively. They are willing to learn new things, and they often find that their kids will teach them what they need to know. They are also wrestling with the age-appropriateness of various boundaries.

Hands Full = able and willing to learn and help kids

Application

After you identify which type of high-tech parent you are, you can approach this subject honestly and begin to move in a positive direction. You will be surprised how much you will learn and become comfortable with.

Addictions

Unfortunately, young teens and preteens are not very good at balancing the good things in their lives. I remember coming home from high school football practice and eating an entire bag of Doritos and drinking a couple of bottles of Yoo-Hoo. I remember watching three movies in a row on summer nights. I remember playing video games for six hours straight. None of that was unusual for me or my friends. Kids, by nature, are much more impulsive, much less logical, and much less educated about the consequences of their behavior. They do because they can, and they don't truly believe that there can ever be too much of a good thing. They believe that if a little bit of a video game (or Doritos or Mountain Dew or Red Bull) is good, then a whole lot of it is great. Adolescents are not known for their superior and consistent judgment.

This is where we, the adults, need to get involved and discuss the consequences of electronic addictions. But first, we need to understand the power of teenage addictions—that teens are far more prone to addictive behavior, and that their brains record those good feelings intensely and permanently. The addictions become the default buttons in the brain, so that when the child grows older, those addictions come back again and again. In other words, a teen who is addicted to something will feel that pull toward that particular addiction throughout his or her life.

A few years ago I heard someone on the radio refer to this generation of teens as the "children of the screen." The idea is that kids are spending the vast majority of their free time in front of televisions, movies, computer monitors, cell phones, video games, iPods, and more. The sum of the hours the average teen spends looking at screens is staggering: most studies put it at about forty hours per week, and a 2010 study calculated an even higher rate of play: "Given the amount of time they spend using more than one medium at a time, today's youth pack a total of 10 hours and 45 minutes worth of media content into those daily 7.5 hours—an increase of almost 2.25 hours of media exposure per day over the past five years."[1] The American Academy of Pediatrics recommends seven to twelve hours per week.[2] Some teens will even go to bed with their cell phone under their pillow, just in case they get a text message, a Facebook notification, or feel the need to check something on the Internet. This, of course, disrupts sleep patterns, which directly affects a child's attitude, mental capacity, physical energy, and health. There are studies that show a correlation between screen time and all sorts of physical and emotional problems.

One of the problems with so much screen time is that young people live in a multisensory world of "electronica," according to Adam Cox in his article "The Case for Boredom." The electronic feedback is omnipresent.

> The adolescent mind is nowadays so hyper-stimulated that the absence of stimulation—boredom—is unsettling, while the chaos of constant connection is soothingly familiar. A languishing teenager feels irritable and instinctively knows how to rev up: go online, turn on the TV, call someone, text. Continuous stimulation and communication comprise the new normal . . . Electronica has squeezed the boredom out of life. It makes us crave more of what makes us sick, like an addiction.[3]

Our kids, and many young adults, are living in an ADD world, and they have no interest in living any other way. To the plugged-in young mind, quietness and stillness, two things that religions cherish as spiritual necessities, are deafening, awkward, and miserable. Richard Louv does not buy into the idea that high-tech devices are making kids smarter or more capable.

> As the young grow up in a world of narrow yet overwhelming sensory input (from multimedia everything), many of them develop a wired, know-it-all state of mind. That which cannot be Googled does not count. Frank Wilson, professor of neurology at the Stanford University School of Medicine, says, "For a whole generation of kids, direct experiences in the backyard, in the tool shed, in the fields and woods, have been replaced by indirect learning, through machines. These young people are smart, they grew up with computers, they were supposed to be superior— but now we know that something is missing."[4]

Addiction to pornography is a particular problem in the 21st century. It is an epidemic among boys and girls now, and easy accessibility with high-tech devices drives it. For most kids, porn is free, easy to access, and easy to hide. I believe that the vast majority of eighth-grade boys are struggling with pornography, and many are deeply addicted to it already. Various sources have claimed that twelve- to seventeen-year-olds are the largest consumers of Internet pornography.[5] The average age of a child's first exposure to pornography is eleven. A total of 90% of children ages eight to sixteen have viewed pornography online.[6] Studies show that pornography is often a lifelong struggle for those who are exposed to it very early in life, and it often creates other problems in the sexual lives of young adults. Smartphones and tablets, without proper safeguards, make the addiction incredibly accessible, easy to hide, and always available.

Not Your Father's Television

Our culture tends to throw kids into the deep end of the pool without teaching them how to swim. Kids are given adult freedoms and privileges without responsibilities and training. Kids are growing up fast, but not well. Now more than ever, it is essential to give kids age-appropriate responsibilities, privileges, and freedoms.

David Elkind, in his classic book, *The Hurried Child*, wrote about the effects of television on kids:

> Television producers often treat children as grown up . . . Owing in part to watching adults shows on TV, even young children seem quite knowledgeable about the major issues of our time—drugs, violence, crime, divorce, single parenting, inflation, and so on. . . . But exposure is one thing, and understanding is another. Making experiences more accessible does not make them any less confusing or any less disturbing. Ironically, this pseudo-sophistication (the effect of television hurrying children) encourages parents and adults to hurry them even more. But children who sound, behave, and look like adults, nonetheless, still feel and think like children.[7]

Even the relatively tame Disney and Nickelodeon channels, along with the mainstream sitcoms, offer their special blend of grown-up-too-soon. The word for it is *precocious*, and it describes nearly every lead character on shows for tweens. The *New Oxford American Dictionary* defines tween as an adjective meaning "of a child having developed certain abilities or proclivities at an earlier age than usual." The characters on TV, of course, have adult writers crafting their dialogue to make them far more confident, witty, charming, and funny than their ages would otherwise grant. And the plot lines have them involved in an exciting blend of youthful and adult activities and relationships, usually with no parents around. If parents are around, they are portrayed as goofy, unintelligent dorks.

One of the most confusing areas of growing up is sexuality, and there are plenty of mixed messages in every corner of pop culture. Elkind writes,

> The media encourages sexual expression at just the age children should be learning some healthy repression . . . . Part of growing up is learning to control impulses and to behave morally . . . The real danger of growing up fast is that children may learn the rules of social license before they learn the rules of social responsibility.[8]

Media is changing the images and expectations of childhood, both for children and for adults. Television has changed the norms. Kids seem to vault immediately from carefree innocence to all the rights and privileges of adulthood. And we must remember that twelve- to fourteen-year-olds are extremely impressionable; they are watching and evaluating everything, even the ads.

"Advertisers hurry children into psychologically and nutritionally unhealthy consumerism," according to Elkind. For every twenty-two minutes of TV programming, there are eight minutes of advertisements, so this is no small thing. And of course, nearly every website, video game, and DVD has plenty of ads for the kids. The purpose of every ad is to manipulate viewers to think that they need something the advertisers are selling, and kids are poorly equipped to manage these subtle, powerful messages.

Therefore, children should not be given free reign of the cable television, computer, tablet, or smartphone. Parents need to establish age-appropriate limits on channels, shows, and viewing time. Less is better, in general, but with proper guidance and boundaries, television can be a good teacher. Kids can learn a tremendous amount of history, science, and literature from high-quality programs.

Some of the best tools for guiding children's television experiences are parental controls, the DVR, Netflix, and the Off button. I highly recommend using of all those tools. In our family, AT&T U-Verse has worked well because of its excellent parental controls and the DVR. We have cut cable for long periods of time and used an antenna and Netflix streaming on a Roku. Our kids cannot watch whatever they want. We have rules and guidelines, and we monitor what is on. We enjoy the best programming we can get and we skip commercials as much as possible. You and your family can find your own way. It is possible, now more than ever, to control what comes into your house, but it takes a hands-on approach.

The Trouble with Video Games

I am not a gamer, but I have played enough video games in my life to know that they're awesome, especially for a young boy or girl who craves adventure and a place to exercise imagination and mental prowess. Video games offer the most multisensory, stimulating, interactive, and social activity that a young boy or girl can experience. Most games require hand-eye coordination, sharp timing, and a keen sense of problem-solving. Many games involve communicating with other players using a headset microphone, and most kids will tell you that they love to play in small groups even more than they like to play alone. For many kids, it is the most fun way to interact with their peers. They play together, then they laugh, tease, and brag about the games they played.

It is hard to compete with all those sights, sounds, and vibrations, especially when the child has the omnipotence to start, restart, and stop the experience at will. And when a game gets a little stale, a new and different one can be easily borrowed or bought. It is entirely convenient, highly personal, and completely controllable, unlike real-life experiences like pursuing a new friend, reading a book, or going fishing.

What I love about video games is that they can be a very social activity for boys and girls to play—*between more active, creative activities*. Sometimes my son and I will play a game when we are wiped out from the other activities of the day and we just want to chill out and have some fun. We tease each other and laugh a lot as we play a game that keeps us acting and reacting to each other's onscreen moves. Mostly, he wins, which makes him feel great, but most importantly, we enjoy the free-spirited competition—the laughs, the taunts, the punches—much more than the game itself.

As with every good thing, there can be too much of it. Moderate amounts of time, money, and love for video games must be maintained for the good of the children. If you deliberately limit the resources devoted to video games, they can be a fun part of a healthy family.

The other aspect of moderation is the content of the games. Although there are many wonderful games that expand players' imaginations and problem-solving skills, there are some major concerns to consider.

Violence

Violence is rampant and graphic on television, but for the most part it is found in the crime dramas that adults watch. Violence in video games, on the other hand, is not only rampant and graphic, but it is found in the games kids play most, and tremendous visceral rewards and points are granted for committing extreme violence. We are no longer just defeating or dissolving an opponent, but now we are often graphically and brutally mangling him to death. In some cases, torture and dismemberment are applauded and rewarded.

To be clear, I am not opposed to all video-game violence. Many boys and girls are itching for an adventure, a quest, or a battle to fight, and the modern world does not allow much of that outside of football, hockey, hunting, and a few other highly physical full-contact activities, many of which are not accessible to most kids. So our boys, in particular, need an outlet for their primal urges to protect, to explore, to strategize, to hunt, and to fight. Some video games provide a healthy outlet for those natural feelings. I look for games in which the player is fighting for good against evil, using strategy and wisdom to solve problems and avoid disaster. I look for games that require restraint as much as sheer power and aggression. The problem is that those games are hard to find. I think the Halo and Fable games generally fit the criteria, but many parents will find them too violent. I think they are great for twelve years and up in moderation. The LEGO series of video games is truly outstanding for younger players aged six to twelve. Common Sense Media is an excellent source for information on the good games out there; the lists change monthly, so refer to the website.

Mayhem

Many games portray drug use, prostitution, driving over pedestrians, beating up bystanders, vandalism, and so on. Check the labels and research online.

Profanity

Why there is not a "disable profanity" option on all games, I will never understand. Anyway, check for it. Often, it just runs quietly in the background. Also, be aware that kids with headsets on may be listening to foul-mouthed abusive bullies on the other end.

Sex

Many games are designed to appeal to teenage boys, so there are characters and situations specifically crafted to titillate that target market, and they're not always right on the cover of the game. Once again, check the online reviews and previews before purchasing.

Age-appropriateness is a very subjective and challenging thing to determine, but we should attempt to make every media choice based on what's acceptable and good for kids at each level of development. That's easier said than done, but it can be done with some help. My favorite place to research media content in general and video-game content in particular is Common Sense Media.

I believe there is a place for video games in the home of the child who is growing up well. Proceed with caution, keep an eye on the screens (including the phones), and have some fun. Join in with the kids for some real laughter. Just don't expect to win.

Move Slowly

New media and social media evolve very quickly, so it is likely that by the time you read this, some of the information and advice will be outdated. Young people move from one social media platform to another in a matter of months, not years, so it's important that we be quick to learn about new technologies and electronics, but slow to adopt them. Avoid the temptation to buy what everybody else is buying for Christmas or for sixth-grade graduation. Postpone. Delay. Go slow. And never allow your children to own anything that you don't understand or don't feel like you can control. Grandma may want to buy your child the new iPhone, but don't allow it until you have fully vetted the pros and cons and made a deliberate choice as a family.

Model Good Behavior

Be sure to moderate your own use of media and to model a healthy, balanced relationship with modern devices. You must avoid your own addictions and continually remind your children that electronic addiction is not an option for anyone in your family, parents included. Parents should not spend their time on the sidelines of a soccer game with their faces in their phones.

Establish Healthy Boundaries

You can establish healthy boundaries for your kids and include the whole family in the conversation. Some families meet to discuss and establish a Family Media Agreement for the home (an example of an FMA is in the Digital Citizenship chapter). Other families may not be comfortable with formal written contracts, but they can establish their own verbal agreements. However you do it, it is crucial to establish healthy practices, such as docking all devices for charging overnight, banning devices at the dinner table, having a digital Sabbath, and keeping Internet-connected devices in public spaces. A few good rules and routines can make all the difference in establishing and maintaining a healthy balance.

Spend Your Time Wisely

Make sure to balance a moderate amount of screen time each week with copious amounts of people time, book time, and nature time. Send those kids outside to play. Take them to the library to borrow some books, magazines, and music. Set up game nights with the neighbors or a favorite family from church. Go shopping for a new bike. Go camping, fishing, hunting, or swimming. Just get the kids involved with people and physical activities so they are moving, playing, and being creative and active. It's not enough to say no to screens. Say yes to the other things that make life an adventure.

Ultimately, we should want our kids to use technology to do good and to be good. We can practice using technology to encourage other people, starting at home. Parents should send kind text messages and funny e-mails to the kids. Share uplifting, interesting articles with each other. Brag about your kids, friends, and other family members on Facebook. Wish people happy birthday with a personalized card of some kind. It is important for kids to know that technology can be used for good or for evil, and that we choose good every time.

Perhaps all of this seems totally overwhelming, but everything worth doing well is worth doing poorly at first. So, humble yourself and start learning. Get involved and do what you can to show your kids that you care, that you are there in their digital world, and that you will not let them drown.

MOBILE DEVICES

When I was a young teenager in the early '80s, the family television was the source of all entertainment and the family telephone was the source of all social communication; it was all based in the living room. There were boxes and cords all over the place. Everything was bulky, disconnected, expensive, and controlled by Mom and Dad. There was no privacy and we kids had to wait our turn to take or make a phone call. Things have changed.

Now, kids' lives revolve around their mobile devices, which are the hub of all things entertaining and social. The really lucky ones have been given smartphones, where every new bit of technology is contained in a single device, and parents make all the payments. These are the most privileged children in the history of the world—and I am not using hyperbole.

Smartphones are all-in-one devices that fit in a kid's pocket. They provide instant access to everything you can imagine:

- Cell phone service
- Text messaging
- Social media (Twitter, Instagram, Snapchat . . .)
- Video games
- Music (Pandora, iTunes, MP3 . . .)
- Videos (YouTube, broadcast TV, cable TV . . .)
- Applications (movies on demand, cable TV channels, gambling games . . .)
- High-definition camera and viewer
- High-definition video camera and player

What kids can do with their smartphones in a matter of seconds with a few clicks or swipes on a touchscreen will blow you away. Try it—go find some teenagers. Ask them to show you something really cool or technologically crazy that their smartphones do. They will think it's funny and will probably enjoy the challenge. If they don't know where to start, then say, "Show me how you can take a picture or video, write a caption, and post it to a social media site where all your friends and their friends can see it." Then note just how long the whole process takes. Or ask them to show you a street view on Google Earth or a game they can play online with their friends. Ask them what they love about their mobile devices. It probably will not take much to get them to open up, if you ask with sincerity and flattery. They like to talk about their devices.

Unfortunately, the smartphone, as with all new waves of technology, is used for evil as well as for good.

"Check this out," says an eleven-year-old boy to his friend as he shows off a series of X-rated websites that can be turned off instantly as an adult approaches. An addiction is born.

"You are not going to believe what she said about you last night," says the twelve-year-old girl to her best friend as she shows her a lengthy string of mean-spirited text messages, e-mails, and postings on social media sites. A girl is humiliated and infuriated.

"You know the new girl in math class? She has these crazy pictures on Instagram and Snapchat," says the thirteen-year-old boy to his friend as they view dozens of sexy pictures the new girl posted to get attention. The boys decide to share these pictures with all their friends; many collect and trade them like their dads used to do with baseball cards. Another reputation is ruined.

"He is so hot. And look at this one. So gross, don't you think?" says the fourteen-year-old girl to her new friend as they peruse photos of boys in their grade using Tinder and Hot or Not, apps that allow local users to rate each other's photos, then connect with them in a chat room.

These scenarios may seem like only the work of the most needy or hardened teens, but this is relatively normal behavior in most neighborhoods around the nation. Most parents and teachers are unaware, since they have no presence in the online world of their children.

In all honesty, many kids with smartphones avoid pornography and cyberbullying, but they are addicted to games and social media. These kids are good kids who spend incredible amounts of time playing age-appropriate games and chatting online with their friends. The amount of time the average kid spends looking at his smartphone is nearly incalculable, since it is constantly going up to face, down to lap, and into pocket in a never-ending waltz. 1–2–3. And 1–2–3. These kids will find it difficult, if not impossible, to spend a day without the devices that have become an integral way of interacting with the world, a sixth sense they don't know how to live without. Just ask a teenager how she would feel if she had to live a week without an Internet-connected device of any kind. Or ask if you can borrow his phone for the day. Most kids would admit quickly and honestly that they would feel naked and unprepared to do life.

Michael Simon says in his book titled *The Approximate Parent*, "Digital media is ever-present and incredibly attractive to teen brains—especially teen brains that register novelty, risk-taking and the feeling of connection as highly pleasurable. The Internet, gaming, and use of social media are addicting."[1] We need to realize that these devices are not just another toy or music player.

My thirteen-year-old son is typically thankful for what he gets and takes good care of his things, but even though most of his friends have had smartphones for a few years (and have never paid a dime of their own money for the privilege), I do not allow him that luxury. I don't think it's a good idea to give a ten- to fourteen-year-old a smartphone, and over time, my son has come to agree with me. He is annoyed by his friends' addictions to their devices and their antisocial behavior as much as I am.

I am not Amish or a Luddite; my boy has a simple cell phone and an iPod, so he is able to do most of the things that an iPhone can do. But I've disabled the iPod's web browser and set up strict parental controls so he can't surf the Internet or watch R-rated content without my permission. And he cannot download an app, song, or video without my password, so that allows me to know what he is buying and consuming. This arrangement allows him to communicate with his friends, play games, and use other miscellaneous apps. Most importantly, he is not an electronics addict, and continues to be happy doing other things, like playing soccer, playing his electric guitar, or playing with his dog.

Digital Citizenship
In this new age of instant information and communication, our parenting responsibility is not just to warn our kids of

danger, but to train them to live in this high-stakes high-tech world of good and evil.

"We live today in a digital echo chamber, in which the most private of moments may be captured in text, photograph, and video, and put online," writes Adam Cohen in reference to the rape case in Steubenville, Ohio. "The victim of a sexual assault can be victimized a second time when images and rumors about her ricochet across her peer group—and a third time when they find a global audience on the Internet. Worse still for victims, the Internet never forgets."[1] The key piece of evidence in the case was the smartphone video. Clearly, smartphones have changed the entire world, and the consequences of abusing these powerful devices continue to escalate. A smartphone can be used as a weapon and will be treated as such in court if it is used to harm a person. It can also be a tool for justice. We must teach our kids to use digital devices for good and never for evil.

Rather than forbidding our young teens from using all mobile devices, we must teach them to view the world as an exciting and wonderful place of beauty and truth that is filled with good people who have so much to teach us. Yet we have to be very careful out there in the online world. By explaining the rules of the road—and the reasons for the rules—kids can think critically in situations where perhaps there is no set rule or when they are just not thinking about the rules.

The bottom line is that parents and teachers must be involved in the digital lives of kids if we're going to help prevent dangerous situations and consequences that could last a lifetime. The kids will not find the right path on their own—that is for certain.

Digital Safety
Of the many dangers high technology presents, the greatest is distracted driving. It is the biggest threat to child

safety, and it is up to parents to avoid every temptation to text or call while driving. Hand the phone to your child or another passenger and ask them to do the texting or calling. If you are alone, think of the safety of the others on the road. Better yet, take the call or send the text later—or just pull off the road.

Families are also threatened by identity theft and other Internet-related crimes. Change your passwords at least once per year, strengthen them, and keep them in a safe place. And for several reasons, do not let your kids know your passwords, because they might make mistakes that affect the whole family. It is important to regularly update (or auto-update daily) all anti-virus, anti-spam, and other security programs on all digital devices. Check your privacy settings on all social media sites. These steps are a hassle, but an ounce of prevention is worth a pound of cure.

A dangerous little function of mobile devices that more and more apps and websites are using is the location finder. Most social media sites have a feature that tells the world where you are, and many people love it. The problem is that it essentially provides all the information a thief or stalker would ever want about you and your kids. Avoid using these whenever possible, and do not tell the world on Facebook or Twitter that you are out of town on vacation for a week, or even where you are going tonight. That information could get into the hands of someone— maybe a friend of a friend, or your handyman's roommate—who will show up to clean out your house while you're gone. Also, realize that your children could be giving constant updates to their friends about exactly where they are at all times, and a stalker could be watching through social media. Child abductions are very rare, but other crimes are possible with social media updates that shout to the world "Here I am!" all the time.

However, the "find my phone" feature built into most phones (and other location apps) can help you locate your young teen. This is not just a safety tool but a nice way of knowing whether they are where they say they are. If they said they were going to the mall, then they should not be at a friend of a friend's house for a party. The app can help you know.

Piracy, or illegal downloading, is rampant among middle school kids, who steal music, movies, and all sorts of intellectual property because it's so easy and enforcement is so rare. This is an issue of integrity, and it's a great opportunity to talk with kids about paying an honest wage to the artists who create the music, movies, and games that we love. Explain that if the content is free, like on Pandora and many other websites, advertisers are paying for it, but ultimately, we should at some point pay for our favorite artists' works. Piracy is stealing, and it is dishonest, even if everybody is doing it.

Cheating is another problem that new media exacerbates for early adolescents, who have lots of ways to share answers online. Many, many students commit plagiarism by cutting and pasting from the Internet instead of writing their own papers, and even more use Google to find answers to workbooks and textbooks. Plenty of students don't see anything wrong with reading a few chapters of an assigned book and then going to SparkNotes (a modern-day online CliffsNotes, basically) to read the summaries and analysis. They tell themselves that they read the book—just not completely. Some kids graduate without ever reading a whole book; I've met a few who were proud of that great accomplishment.

These examples are just the tip of the iceberg. Keep this in mind as your children write book reports and essays. Talk with them about the books and ask them not to use SparkNotes. Keep an eye out for websites that give answers. Check the Internet history every week or so and look out for cheating tools.

Teens often feel a sense of anonymity online, and they feel empowered by the technology to say things they would not say to someone in person. This leads to all sorts of horrible bullying and retaliation in kind. Let's just say that things can turn truly evil in a hurry online. For example, one piece of gossip or just one lie can cause a firestorm of online social drama.

Some claim that cyberbullying—willful psychological harm inflicted through the use of digital devices—is much more prevalent today than stranger danger, because the threat is coming from our kids' peers. But no matter how common it is, it should not be tolerated. We cannot just blow it off with a boys-will-be-boys attitude. Cyberbullying should be reported to authorities. Children must be taught to take a screenshot of the offensive material and show it to a parent, school official, or police officer.

We need to make sure our kids know that words and imagery get passed along, and will make their way to exactly the wrong person. Teach kids to be extremely careful with what they put online, especially on social media. Every word and image made with a digital device should be treated as public and permanent.

Social Media Tips

1. Delay all social media involvement as long as possible. I recommend not allowing any Facebook, Twitter, Instagram, Snapchat, Google+, or any others (and they are continually evolving) until a child is fourteen. At that point, ease into them slowly. This may seem puritan, but I've worked full-time for twenty years with middle school children, and I know that most young teens struggle to survive the school lunchroom. What makes us think they can handle the bare-knuckle, no-holds-barred arena of social media? Delay, then ease in with guidance.

2. When the time comes, parents should have full access to every account, password, and friendship their kids have on every social media site. It might be best to have the kids share an account with Mom or Dad while they learn the rules of the road, like a driver's permit. Granting children total online privacy is a very bad idea, no matter what anyone says. Also, be sure to carefully set each site's settings for security. By default, they are all set for total openness, which makes for a scary lack of privacy.

3. Make sure your children never, ever "friend" someone online who they do not know personally. Every online social connection must correspond with a real friendship in the real world. And personal information should never be given online that wouldn't be given face to face.

4. Remind children often that every picture, every message, and everything that is done online may stay online forever, and can be taken as a screenshot and forwarded in an instant. There is no such thing as online privacy, and the Internet remembers everything, so kids must proceed with great caution.

5. Make sure that every mobile device and computer has a password-protected lock on the home screen. This ensures that their friends cannot pose as them or steal any of their pictures.

6. Let your kids know that if anything happens online that is strange or upsetting in any way, they need to tell a parent, who can determine how to handle it best. Transparency and trust are a must.

7. Be "friends" with your child online, but do not post comments and pictures for their friends to see. Be cool. Just watch and learn. Limit your

online communications with them to texting and e-mailing. E-mail them funny and informative things that they will like. Let them know that you are there, that you care, and that you love them. Send them good news, encouraging messages, and inside jokes regularly.

8. Allow absolutely no social media late at night. Set a time, perhaps 8:00 P.M., when all devices are turned off and returned to the family docking station in the kitchen or the parents' bedroom. All screens should be shut down at least thirty minutes before bedtime to make it easier to fall asleep.

9. Have a digital Sabbath now and then, when the whole family turns off all devices for a day, or a half day at least. If your children struggle with wanting to check their online lives during these times, then it's time to cut back. Same for you. Get outside, if possible.

Digital Manners

On a recent local radio talk show, the host proclaimed, "I think smartphones are the most disruptive devices ever invented to family life. They are wedges between family members. Just look at families at restaurants now. At least one, if not all of them are on their phones. Instead of filling in the silences with conversation, people go to right to their phones." Perhaps this is a bit of hyperbole, since not every family is technologically dysfunctional, but on the whole I have to agree that many—if not most—families are not managing their mobile devices well.

Certainly, without observing digital-device etiquette, we are missing opportunities to relate to the real people in our lives, and in many cases, we are offending them. So put away the phones, tablets, and other electronic devices during meals and meetings, at the very least. Make that a family habit. And do not ever be afraid to tell a young teenager to put a device away. They need to be taught not to choose screens over people's faces and voices, and that nobody should feel that we love our devices more than we love them. With practice and with good role models, kids can develop good digital manners.

Digital citizenship is not simple, and kids will not pick it up on their own. They will require guidance off and on for many years. The following are some well-designed agreements that have been created and tested by experts. Take them and rewrite them with your family in mind to make them your own. You might want to simplify them to a more memorable, concise list. You could write one for each member of the family. Maybe have a child illustrate them. But whatever you do, be sure to discuss them as a family and sign them, then post them in a public space and refer to them as problems arise. As time goes on and kids mature, they should be revisited and revised as necessary. They should be living documents that encourage ongoing discussions between children and their parents.

Family Media Agreements
Because digital citizenship is not simple and kids will not pick it up on their own, it can be helpful to rely on a Family Media Agreement for guidance. Below are some well-designed agreements that have been created and tested by experts. Take them and rewrite them with your family in mind, perhaps simplifying one to make a more memorable, concise list. You could write one for each member of the family, and maybe have the kids illustrate them. But whatever you do, be sure to discuss them as a family, then sign them and post them in a public space, where you can refer to them as problems arise. As time goes on and your kids mature, you can revisit and revise the agreements as necessary. Each one should be a living document that encourages ongoing discussion between children and parents.

For more examples, search for "family media agreement" on my blog at www.growingupwell.org.

The Parent's Pledge

1. I will make sure that my children handle media consumption in a responsible, balanced way that reflects our family values. I will make sure their screen time is limited so they do not become addicted to it.

2. I promise to teach my children when and how to use various communication methods to interact with others. I will make sure my children never forget that digital information travels fast and far and can be saved forever by anyone. I will teach my children that anything they post online is public and permanent.

3. I will help everyone in our family understand that our technology usage affects others, including family, friends, and all the communities to which we belong.

4. I will get to know the services and websites my children use. If I do not know how to use them, I will take the time to learn how. I will try to be interested in and learn about what my children enjoy online.

5. I will try to get to know my children's online friends just as I try get to know their other friends. I will help my children understand they need to always act the way they want to be treated and that they should not respond to bullying online.

6. I will teach my children that some material that is available online is intellectual property, and is protected and cannot be taken without permission.

7. I will spend time teaching my children to protect their technology and data from viruses, spyware and adware, and I will install content filters on the web browsers they use. I will also show that having protection such as secure passwords is important for all technology.

8. I will not just make rules as a parent, but I will have conversations with my child about what I feel is best for him or her.3

I agree to the above.

Parent's signature: _____

I understand that my parent has agreed to these rules and I agree to help my parent explore and use technology with me.

Child's signature: _____

Adapted in part from SafeKids.com and from and the "Family Media Agreement: 6–8" from Common Sense Media.3, 5

Kids' Pledge

1. I will remember that I need to balance technology use with other activities. I will pursue much more than a digital life. I will pursue people and activities that are healthy for me. I will cooperate with my parents as they help me manage my screen time to a healthy, moderate level.

2. I understand that whatever I share online or on my cell phone can travel far and fast and can be saved permanently; therefore, I will be extremely cautious about what I post online.

3. I will tell my parents if I experience any emotional pain or discomfort when using technology.

4. I will not respond to any messages that are mean or in any way make me feel uncomfortable. It is not my fault if I get a message that is not appropriate. If I do, I will tell my parents or a responsible adult right away so that they can help me deal with the problem.

5. I will treat others the way I wish to be treated when using technology. I will keep in mind that my technology use affects others and that messages do not always get erased or forgotten.

6. I will check with my parents before downloading music or installing software or doing anything that could possibly hurt our computer or jeopardize my family's privacy. I will also keep programs such as anti-virus, spyware and adware up to date to protect our information, and I will use at least a moderate filter on my Internet browser at all times.

7. I will not create any accounts or give out any private information, such as my full name, date of birth, address, phone number or photos, without my parents' permission. I will not share passwords with anyone, even my best friends.

8. I will be a good online citizen and not do anything that hurts other people or is against the law, including copyright laws. This includes plagiarizing and downloading any media (music, movies, books, etc.) without paying the appropriate fees.

9. I will help my parents understand how to have fun and learn things online and teach them things about the Internet, computers and other technology.4

I agree to the above.

Child's signature: _____

I will help my child follow this agreement and will allow reasonable use of digital technology as long as these rules and other family rules are followed.

Parent's signature: _____

Adapted in part from the brochure "Child Safety on the Information Highway" by Lawrence J. Magid and the "Family Media Agreement: 6–8" from Common Sense Media.4, 5

OUTDOOR LIFE

I go into nature to be soothed and healed and to have my senses put in tune once more.

—John Burroughs

Stress reduction, greater physical health, a deeper sense of spirit, more creativity, a sense of play, even a safer life—these are the rewards that await a family when it invites more nature into children's lives.

—Richard Louv

On vacation in Destin, Florida, my extended family and I—all fourteen of us—spent each day building sandcastles, playing in the waves, and cooking seafood. In contrast, it seemed like all the other teenagers we saw, especially the girls, spent their vacations walking along the beach with their smartphones in their faces, oblivious to the wonder of the ocean and the interesting people around them.

Statistics support the notion that screens are ruling teens; kids spend well over forty hours per week in front of electronic screens, but less than forty minutes per week in nature.

Delayed Gratification

A major component of growing up is learning to deal with long waits and unexpected delays, yet nearly everything is now available in an instant. Instant messaging. On-demand movies. Instant-winner lottery tickets. Ultra-fast food. Five-minute total-body workouts. You name it, and we can find a way to fit more into our days. And with the average smartphone, people don't need to waste any downtime for any reason. Every spare second gets filled.

Mature adults learn that many of the best things in life take a long time to develop. A great education takes twenty years. A rock-solid, happy marriage takes a good decade to develop. A garden is made over the course of many months of daily tending. Hunting and fishing take tremendous patience and skills honed over years of practice.

If we are going to prepare our kids for the best things in life, we need to teach them to wait and reward them for being patient. Kids need opportunities to practice patience that are followed by rewards for sticking with it to the end—whether it's a 500-piece puzzle or a friendship with a neighbor that takes a long time to develop.

Once again, the push-button culture is working against kids. They are constantly given immediate, customized, positive feedback from their cell phones, iPods, video games, YouTube, and Facebook. These are places where they can hit pause, fast-forward, or reset any time they like with no consequences. But in real life, and especially in the natural world, there are no fast-forward or reset buttons. In order to experience a sunset, you have to watch for a while. A computer cannot simulate that experience.

The Need for Nature

Richard Louv, author of the best-selling book *Last Child in the Woods*, understands this problem more than anyone, and loves children enough to cry out for them, "Let the children play outdoors!" His books and lectures have inspired a national movement that wants to leave no child inside. He encourages all families to embrace the nature that is in their local community. "For children," he writes, "nature comes in many forms. A pet that lives and dies; a worn path through the woods; a fort nested in stinging nettles—whatever shape nature takes, it offers each child an older, larger world separate from parents. Nature offers healing for a child."[1]

Louv explains how our children's generation is suffering from what he calls "nature deficit disorder," a preventable ailment of the body, mind, and soul. Kids just don't go outdoors anymore. Just look out the window and count the children; most likely the only people you see are older people walking dogs or taking out the trash. Louv's book opens with a telling quote by a fourth grader in San Diego who said, "I like to play indoors better 'cause that's where all the electric outlets are."

Electronic screens are more like screen doors or screen windows than windows onto the real world. We can see and hear things through them to some extent, but the clarity and depth perception are inferior. We're not fully in the world, even though we can hear and see and maybe even feel some of what's happening out there. These digital doorways are virtual experiences at best; we need to get out into reality more. Our children, especially, deserve to be outdoors more.

Richard Louv explains that a child's healthy mental and emotional development depend on outdoor experiences. "Nature inspires creativity in a child by demanding visualization and the full use of the senses. . . . Nature can frighten a child, too, and this fright serves a purpose. In nature, a child finds freedom, fantasy, and privacy: a place distant from the adult world, a separate peace."[2] To sum up, a child who spends time outdoors in nature will be stronger and more capable than the typical indoor child.

Go Outside and Don't Come Back Until . . .

Many of us grew up hearing our parents say, "Go outside and don't come back until six for dinner." We knew we had to go find something, anything to do. It might be shooting hoops next door, building a fort in the woods nearby, riding our bikes to the grocery store, or starting up a game of capture the flag or two-hand-shove football. Some of us would play video games in the basement of a friend's house, especially when the weather was lousy, but generally, we played outdoors. In direct contrast, most of today's kids are indoors, have no desire to go out, and have parents who are afraid that it's just too dangerous out there.

So, what do we do to get our kids and the neighbors' kids outdoors? First, we should send them out the way our parents and grandparents did. Tell them, "Get out of here. Go play. Make some fun out there." If they will not budge off the couch, then take the remote controls or handheld devices and say that they can have them back after they play outside for an hour. Just do not let them sit inside all afternoon. If they're engrossed in a book, tell them to take it outside. Just move them, one way or another, outdoors. But do not be too specific about what they need to do outside. If they want to nap, they can nap in the hammock. As long as they are getting some fresh air and sunshine, be happy. Give them freedom out there.

Second, we can participate. We can throw a Frisbee, toss a baseball, or shoot baskets. We can pump up the bike tires, dust off the helmets, get rolling. We can set up a kickball game in the cul-de-sac or common ground. It is not a two-hour commitment. It is just a "prime the pump" sort of thing. We can get them started, then we can go back to the house to get things done. Or just play. Sometimes we need to play as much as the kids do.

Third, buy equipment that promotes outdoor play. Invest in gear that neighbor kids and school friends will want to use. It can be as simple and affordable as a box of balls, cones, Wiffle bats, Frisbees, and sidewalk chalk, or as elaborate and expensive as a swimming pool. Consider the investment in dollars per use over the years, as well as the value of having your kids outdoors and having their friends at the house, where you can supervise and get to know them. Consider setting aside a big chunk of money for a backyard budget, and then discuss with all the kids in the family the best way to spend it so they'll have as much fun as possible outdoors.

Finally, invite kids over. So often, there are kids nearby who would love to play outside, but they need to be invited. In the old days, you didn't have to invite them, but now you do. Get outside and knock on some doors. Have a plan for a game and then recruit kids to play. Once they have a good time, they can recruit others. Soon enough, you may have one of those neighborhoods where the kids know each other and play together long into the summer nights. Invite their parents to participate or to come over for a happy hour in your lawn chairs. Most people find it wonderfully refreshing, but they need to be invited outdoors. Your neighborhood can be one where the kids play together and the adults talk to each other. They do exist, but they are intentionally created.

How to Turn Kids On To Nature

The best way we can unhook kids from their screens is to get them hooked on something even more interactive and real. What better antidote for digital addiction than fishing, hiking, or hunting? Now, not everybody has the ability or desire to hunt, fish, hike, or camp, but most people can do something beyond their neighborhood, out in the wild, even if it is just taking a walk in the woods. Go take a walk in the hour before the sun goes down, when many animals, even deer, are likely to be moving around. The morning hours are great for seeing birds and squirrels on the move. And you don't have to go way out in the country. A big city park or a suburban trail will suffice.

Jake Hindman, an outdoor education center supervisor with the Missouri Department of Conservation and a true outdoorsman₃, travels around the state teaching adults how to get kids interested in the outdoors. Here is a summary of his three-point lecture:

Prepare
Go overboard in prepping for a day on the lake or in the woods. It is not about you—at all. It is all about fun and making good memories. You have to set aside your self and focus on the kids. Do not plan on fishing. Be the guide. Be the entertainer, the host. Make sure you have bug spray, favorite snacks, fun music for the road trip, and anything else that can make the day special, like catching your first fish, and free of problems like bug bites. Bring walkie-talkies, some fireworks, paintball guns, or water balloons. Just make sure the kids have a good time and that they are safe. Even if the fishing is a failure, being outdoors can still be a blast.

All of that takes forethought, shopping, and packing at least a day in advance. In fact, the prep work may take more time and energy than the outdoor adventure itself, but it's the most important thing of all.

Patience
Do not push too hard. Let the experience flow on its own. Keep your experiences short and sweet. Leave before the kids are tired, hungry, or cranky. Leave the party while you're still having fun. Again, this is not about what you want to do. You are the host. Make sure all the kids have fun, and in the end, you will end up having a great time,

too. One great hour outdoors with kids is better than a whole day of bad experiences. Keep it short and sweet.

Praise

Celebrate every little success. Exaggerate your excitement about every little thing that you see as good. Take the good and make it seem great. Putting a worm on a hook for the first time should get a high five. Catching a fish should get photographed. Retell the events of the day with enthusiasm. Brag about it for days. Put the pictures on the fridge.

Taking Johnny to the Woods

My son invited his buddy Johnny to join us on our day trip to the woods. Johnny is a hockey player who plays video games, does well in school, and lives a typical suburban lifestyle. He had never spent much time in the woods and had never shot a firearm, so this little trip would be a new experience.

From the time we picked him up at his dad's house on Saturday morning to the moment we arrived in the woods, Johnny played with his iPod and said nothing unless he was directly asked a question. There was no life in him until we showed him how to shoot a shotgun safely—and then he hit half the clay pigeons we threw for him. Then he and my son spent a few hours exploring the creek and damming up a few pools of water to sit in on that hot day.

On the way home, Johnny was energized. He wouldn't stop talking and his iPod was nowhere to be seen. The boys chatted the whole way home, full of life.

I have seen this before. Kids who spend a lot of time in front of screens are far less social and show much less imagination than those who play in unstructured settings. But when you get them on the lake or in the woods, they warm up quickly and come alive.

The key to that day was that it was all planned with the kids in mind: the time of departure (later than normal), the order of activities, the snacks and lunch. I spent the day teaching, supervising, and running the activities. I gave the boys some ideas about what to do in the creek, but then I let them do their own thing. And we left the woods while we were still having fun so the next trip would be eagerly anticipated.

The next time we took Johnny to the woods, he left his iPod and headphones at home and had a great time from start to finish without a single electronic device. He knew it was going to be a real-world adventure.

You do not have to be a camo-wearing outdoorsman to enjoy nature; on the next page are some ideas for all sorts of people who are willing to get outside with their kids. go biking.

take a walk (it's the best way to talk)

go camping (start in your backyard)

play four square

go canoeing

have a picnic at a local lake

go boating, skiing, tubing

stargaze

play in the rain

jump in puddles

garden

ride horses on a trail

fly a kite

fill a birdfeeder

go on a treasure hunt in the woods

play with the hose

wash bikes and sports gear

wash cars for cash

climb a tree

go apple-picking at a local orchard

make a slip-and-slide in the backyard

rake leaves for fun

rake leaves for profit

play in the leaves

play in the sprinkler

walk someone's dog

jog to get in shape for a sport

kick a soccer ball

throw a baseball

shoot hoops

build a snowman or snow cave

go sledding

have a snowball fight

make snow angels

shovel snow for cash

take a nap in a hammock

sleep under the stars on the patio

WORK AND MONEY

"Youth entitlement seems to have reached epidemic proportions in both my family and in society as a whole."

—Kay Wills Wyma

Preparing for Independence

Many eighteen- to twenty-eight-year-old men and women are stuck in adolescence and having nervous breakdowns as they confront their inability to deal with the trials of life. Many are crippled socially and emotionally in the adult world. These young people's parents, teachers, and coaches may have done a fine job of protecting and providing for them, but they did not impart the skills the kids would need for a mature adulthood.

A young child must be protected and nurtured in absolutely every way. He must be fed, clothed, changed, transported, and even cajoled into sleep, or he will get sick and possibly die. Toddlers are totally unprepared for life, so parents must anticipate and meet their every need. But that same child, eighteen years later, should not be helpless or needy. Instead, he should be a strong, self-sufficient young man, able to learn on his own at school, have healthy relationships, and be able to do work that other adults require of him. After all, he is a legal adult, with all the rights and privileges that come with working, paying taxes, pursuing further education, voting, getting married, having children, and even fighting in a war.

It is not easy to prepare kids for independence, but it is possible, and doing it well is giving them a gift for a lifetime and for posterity. As kids develop, we can slowly reduce the protection and provision while we increase the preparation. In the middle school years, our kids can learn to do adult tasks.

Kay Wills Wyma, author of the outstanding book *Cleaning House,* admits, "With the greatest of intentions and in the name of love, we have developed a tendency to race in to save, protect from failure, arrange for success, overprotect, and enable our kids. I decided that my new message needed to be something more along these lines: 'I love you. I believe in you. I know what you are capable of. So I am going to make you work.'"[1]

Preparing young people to become more responsible and skilled will not be easy, but it will be rewarding. The following list is a set of guidelines to point them in the right direction.

Serve Others
We owe our children the wisdom that we have gained about how to work. We owe them the understanding that they can be extremely helpful to others when they use their skills and labor for a good cause. If we begin the process in early adolescence, when we still have great influence on them, we can teach them that they make the world a better place and that they are valuable to their family, friends, and co-workers when they display a strong work ethic and service toward others. We can teach them that we serve

because it helps others, and that it makes us better people. Living a good life includes serving and being served by others.

We can teach them that service is not an event. It is not a project. It is not serving food to homeless people one day a year. It is not writing a check once a year to the United Way. It is a lifestyle. It is just what we do. It is who we are. We pick up after each other. We cook and clean for each other. We do each other's laundry. Service is a vital part of being a family. We serve.

Real Work
Kids need real work. They will sense if they are given busy work that is not important to anyone, so give them real responsibilities as much as possible. They should sense that their work is important and that a job well done is greatly valued—and that shoddy or incomplete work is a problem for others.

Give kids tasks every day around the house that are age-appropriate and legitimately helpful to others, then verbally reward them for sticking with it and doing a good job. Jobs such as emptying and loading the dishwasher, setting the table, and taking out the trash are legitimately helpful, meaningful tasks that children ages ten to fourteen can easily manage.

It should be totally normal for our kids to do helpful tasks. They should expect to hear us say, "Hey, Jen, go get some paper towels from the basement. Thanks." It should not shock them to hear us say, "David, I need you to do the dishes sometime in the next thirty minutes. Thanks." That should be entirely normal.

Parents should not always be working harder than the kids. Kids should often be working with their parents, not watching TV while Mom and Dad do all the preparing and cleaning for dinner. Kids working alongside adults brings benefits to everybody involved.

Modern American children do not feel at all compelled to help around the house unless they are taught to do so properly and rewarded for it. Brett and Kate McKay, in their article "How to Get Your Kids to Do Their Chores," discuss the importance of teaching kids to work when our culture does not.

> Anthropologists studying child-rearing across cultures note that in developing societies, children are almost universally eager to help out and be useful. The contributions of children in developing countries can be crucial to their family's survival. But doing chores is still important for kids living in the suburbs of America; while their responsibilities may not be central to the livelihood of their households, they are essential in helping them grow up in an unselfish and well-adjusted way and shaping them into fully functioning adults and contributing members of society.[2]

Author Mark Gregston, on his podcast "The Family Citizen," seems to agree. He explains that our kids need to feel that their work around the house is necessary.

> Unfortunately, many of today's teenagers make no meaningful contribution to their families. They have nothing more to contribute to the family than reluctantly taking out the garbage or picking up their room after being told again and again. That's not a contribution. At that point it is more like self-preservation . . . Kids need to be given responsibilities in the family that they can claim and make happen without parental badgering. It builds a sense of value and belonging. Kids who make no meaningful contribution to the family tend to grow up feeling entitled and self-absorbed, making them rotten spouses, parents, and citizens as well.[3]

It takes intention to create a family that works together well. At one point, my family was spending so much time traveling to and from sporting events and practices and watching games that none of us had time for our work around the house. When we adjusted our schedules to make more time at home, we created a much healthier, happier family life. It was not easy to make the changes, but it was better for us all.

Allowance

I suggest providing an allowance in return for some chores, but not all of them. Children should do some work without pay simply because they are members of the family, sharing in the blessings of a home, food, clothing, and so on. However, some of the more challenging chores should earn a fair wage. And if the work is not accomplished as agreed upon, then the pay should be reduced accordingly. Nothing motivates kids more than reduced wages for services not rendered.

Children should know that Mom and Dad value a big job done well. We should pay kids to be the house cleaners or the lawn service, and pay them well. Why not pay your own family with your own money? Do not be cheap when it comes to the labor of your child, or you will end up teaching them the work is not worth the money and that Mom and Dad are tightfisted. Paying kids well for hard work teaches them to be generous and fair and helps them understand the value of a dollar. Most kids raised like this will not waste their hard-earned money, and they will not have an inflated sense of entitlement.

Valuable Family Jobs

- mop floors
- clean bathrooms
- dust blinds
- wash the dog
- mow the lawn

- pull weeds
- wash windows
- rake leaves
- shovel snow
- change bedding

Shun Materialism

Parents do not intend to spoil their children rotten. It happens naturally and has subconscious motivation, and our culture encourages it and discourages self-control with money and material goods. It's a material world.

So how do we raise kids who do not feel entitled to a life of ease and luxury? How do we avoid spoiling them to the point where they do not feel the need to work hard, learn new things, and aspire to a productive career?

For starters, we need to buy less stuff—not only for our kids but also for ourselves. We need to shop less and buy less, for the good of the children. They should not grow up thinking that shopping is a hobby. For the spoiled, when the going gets tough, the tough go shopping; kids learn this behavior directly from their parents, and the culture reinforces it, but it's a sure road to entitlement, and I urge you to avoid it.

Instead, we should teach our kids that money is used for all sorts of good. When we make good money, that is a very good thing, but it is not what makes life rich. We can see money and possessions as necessary and good things, but we need to teach that money does not make us happy. While it provides some opportunity for some happiness, the best things in life are not bought with cash or credit.

We should be in the habit of giving away possessions we do not use anymore and recognizing that others can benefit a great deal from our surplus. Let's not store and collect things (dare I say hoard?), but rather share our bounty. And we should expect our kids to give of their own excess, especially at Christmas and birthdays as new gifts come in.

Embrace Work

Work is good: that is the key component of the Protestant work ethic, which has built advanced civilizations. The idea is that God created work because it is good for the soul, good for humanity, and good for the world.

Many people despise work. They view it as a necessary evil and are merely working for the weekend. But work can be good because it uses our body, mind, and talents to create, fix, and solve problems, and to help other people. A great parent will teach his child such an appreciation for work and will model it as best he can. He will be thankful for the opportunities that a good job provides, and will take advantage of opportunities to advance toward more satisfying, rewarding work.

Great parents will explain that, as a family, we work to help each other, to maintain a pleasant home, to earn money, to be healthy, and to enjoy life together. This includes some hard work: cleaning, organizing, cooking, laundering, paying bills, researching, scheduling, communicating, and so forth. It is who we are. We take pride in working hard and doing our jobs well. Make sure that you don't do all your work in an office or back room. Work in the same room with your children so they can see it and learn to appreciate it.

Have a routine for chores. Do housecleaning together as a family every Saturday afternoon, or whatever works for you. Play music loudly and make it fun. And pay well, when it is appropriate.

Praise your kids for a job well done, and correct them when they do a job poorly. Be very patient with them, especially at first.

Be Charitable

Nobody sets out to raise selfish children. It just happens—unless you intentionally create a culture of generosity. By being a good role model for your children and giving them opportunities to give to others, you can help them discover the deep joy of charity. Let's look at some ways to go about this.

Give money to the needy, and make it routine for your kids to give about ten percent of their income to people in great need. Why ten percent? The Judeo-Christian tradition teaches that ten percent is a minimal amount for a person to give to the less fortunate. This openhanded, rather than tightfisted, attitude about money makes one more generous and thankful. It is good for the giver as much as it is good for the needy. Ten percent is also a good standard for building up savings; teach kids to give ten, save ten, and spend the rest.

Collect money for the poor in a giving jar or piggy bank. Sponsor a child through WorldVision or Compassion International. Support an orphanage in a developing nation. Find a cause that you believe helps people in a significant way, then include those people in your daily prayers. Do not just pay an annual donation and forget about it. Rather, keep them in your mind and prayers throughout the year.

Work for others. Work in an animal shelter, volunteer at Sunday school with the younger children, or rake the leaves of an elderly neighbor. Cook a meal for someone who is dealing with illness and deliver it with your kids. Just do something that is clearly helpful in the eyes of your children. Do not stuff envelopes for a nonprofit or make phone calls for a political party, because kids will not see the importance of that sort of thing. They need tangible, measurable results.

It is best to show our kids that being something we do not only because it is good but also because it is good for us. Our time, m. energy represent us, and giving of them creat᠎ meaning. Our souls are strengthened when we help ᠎ners in need.

Personal Finance 101

Children need to know four things about money: how to earn it, spend it, give it, and save it well. We must be good role models and guide our kids about how to handle money. Here are the foundational issues of personal finance in a nutshell:

Four Pillars of Personal Finance

1. Earn well—Maximize your income. Work toward a better income in the future.

2. Spend carefully—Minimize expenses and avoid debt.

3. Give generously (10%)—Give to the poor, the orphans, the disabled, and the needy.

4. Save wisely (10%)—Make compounding interest work for you.

Once again, the culture offers very poor guidance, to say the least. The media gives us bad role models by reporting on big government and big corporations. Advertisers persuade us to do all the wrong things. Schools do not teach money management, although there is a movement to do so by groups such as EverFi.com. Nevertheless, parents are the best solution.

Parents should feel free to talk about some, but not necessarily all, of the family's financial decisions in front of the children, perhaps at the dinner table or during a long car ride. When making big purchases, do not keep all the research and information to yourself. Include the kids and discuss what you are going to buy and why. Also, be involved in your kids' personal decisions about money. When one of the kids asks for an iPad, the family can talk about it at length.

Show kids the power of compounding interest. Explain it and discuss how some people use it to generate wealth through sound investing. Also discuss how other people are abused by it, as compounding interest on debt is a sure way to stay in the cycle of poverty. If you need help, get a banker friend or find a YouTube video to explain it for you. It should be a very interesting and valuable life lesson.

If your child wants a big-ticket item that you approve of and think is educational or healthy in an athletic or artistic way, then consider splitting the cost. If it is a $500 electric guitar or mountain bike, then offer to match their contribution dollar for dollar. Teach them how to shop for the best deal and get the most for their money.

Discuss the idea of dollars per use of various household items. The cost of an everyday dish, for instance, might be $5, and the number of uses might be 1000, so the cost per use is incredibly low. Now look at the cost of a fine china dish and calculate its cost per use. Do the same with the family car vs. Grandpa's boat. Look at the diamond earrings that Mom rarely wears, and explain that diamonds do not depreciate like cars and boats do. It is a fun game that helps kids make better choices about spending their money.

Sell unwanted items online as a way of practicing simplicity, teaching economics, and generating cash. Put the kids to work researching the value of items and include them in discussions about what to give away and what to sell, about price-setting, shipping costs, and hassles to avoid. Use eBay for small, lightweight, valuable items, such as electronics or collectibles; use Craigslist for bulky items that you don't want to ship, such as a bowling ball or lamp.

Buying and selling will teach all sorts of valuable economic lessons to kids, and the family will make money doing it.

It takes many years for children to grow up well. A great kid is not raised in a month or a season, but over a long time of being loved and guided to wellness. Financial health will not come to fruition at twelve or fourteen, but it can happen prior to launch at eighteen, and that is an investment that will bless them and others for a lifetime.

CONCLUSION

Life without kids is easier and more comfortable than life as a parent. Many times, I long for the good old days before kids. When I look back in the rearview mirror, those fields sure look a lot greener than the rocky, rutted, muddy, messy fields of my current life with middle school kids. I sometimes find myself feeling jealous of younger and older couples who are living without the extended responsibilities and limitations of children. It was pretty nice when my wife and I were DINKs (dual income no kids), but that was then and this is now. Life with my wife is so much richer than the single life.

Sometimes when I ask my wife for a pep talk, she reminds me that children make my life more meaningful, rich, adventuresome, funny, and loving than it used to be. She's right, but it's so easy to forget. Andy Gullahorn writes of this feeling in his song "More of a Man"[1]:

> So I suck in my protruding gut
> On our monthly dinner night
> You're saying something about the kids
> As I watch these young men pass me by.

I remember I was just like them
I was lonely but I called it independent
And if lonesome is what manly is
Baby, I was more of a man back then.

Without a doubt, parenting middle school children is daunting. It consumes my life with my wife. We have very little time for each other or for ourselves, but we recognize that for two decades, our kids' lives are an integral part of our life. We remind ourselves that in just four years, our son will be going to college and we will be begging for the good old days when he was a funny, sweet, fast-growing, sometimes awkward middle school boy. Four years. It is going by so fast.

Parents, take heart. Take hold of your children. Make a connection and give them some guidance. The goal is not to be a perfect parent or to have a perfect child. The parent who strives for perfection will end up collapsing in a heap. Simply move forward with your children. Meet them where they are today, take their hearts, and move forward together. Walk the day's path, deal with the day's troubles, and enjoy the journey as much as possible. Do not wish for someone else's easy life. Embrace your beautiful mess of a life with your child.

No matter how hard it gets, do not disengage. Do not be the dad who feels like his kids are in the way of his dreams. Do not be the mom who regularly drops her kids off anywhere but home so she can do what she wants to with her day. Do not be the dad who does not know his kids' favorite things or the mom who does not listen. Do not be the mom who will not say no to her kids out of fear of upsetting them. Do not be the parent who freaks out at little things that do not matter. Do not be a distant uncle of a father or an out-of-town aunt of a mother.

Do not be a hands-off parent, because children do not raise themselves well. Do not try to be perfect. Just be a parent and be a little better each year. In the long run, you will reap what you sow. If you are not investing in your child now, you will pay for it later, one way or another. Do something—anything—to connect with and guide your child today. Parenting is an adventure of the greatest significance. It is your legacy.

NOTES

CHAPTER 1—BE THE PARENT

1. Christopher DeVinck, *The Power of the Powerless: A Brother's Legacy of Love* (The Crossroad Publishing Company, 2006).

2. Danny Silk, *Loving Our Kids on Purpose: Making a Heart-to-Heart Connection* (Destiny Image, 2006).

CHAPTER 2—THE EARLY YEARS

1. Richard Louv, *Last Child in the Woods: Saving Our Children from Nature-Deficit Disorder* (Workman Publishing, 2008).

2. Paul Tough, *How Children Succeed: Grit, Curiosity, and the Hidden Power of Character* (Houghton Mifflin, 2012).

CHAPTER 3—FAMILIES MATTERS

1. "Forced Family Fun," *The Middle* (ABC, September 11, 2011).

CHAPTER 4—DEFINING ADOLESCENCE

1. Anonymous 8th-grade student, "What is a Middle Schooler?" Given to me by a parent many years ago.

2. Sarge927, comments on "What is growing up?" *Yahoo! Answers*, 2006, http://uk.answers.yahoo.com/question/index?qid=20061 106104916AAsgUPW.

3. Anne Landers, "Maturity is Many Things," *Sun Sentinel*, July 17, 1999, http://articles.sun-sentinel.com/1999–07–17/lifestyle/.

4. Steve Hall, "Top Ten Things You Should Know About Your Middle School Student," Unpublished.

5. Trace Adkins, "You're Gonna Miss This," *American Man: Greatest Hits Volume II* (Capitol, 2008, compact disc).

CHAPTER 5—THE POWER OF CONNECTION

1. Gary Smalley and John Trent, *The Blessing* (Pocket Books, 1990).

CHAPTER 6—TAKING CARE OF YOURSELF

1. Donald Miller, *A Million Miles in a Thousand Years: What I Learned While Editing My Life* (Thomas Nelson, 2009).

2. Ibid.

CHAPTER 7—FEAR LESS

1. Steven Levitt and Stephen Dubner, *Freakonomics: A Rogue Economist Explores the Hidden Side of Everything* (William Morrow Paperbacks, 2009).

2. Lenore Skenazy, *Free-Range Kids: How to Raise Safe, Self-Reliant Children (Without Going Nuts With Worry)* (Jossey-Bass, 2010).

3. Jen Hatmaker, "Brave Moms Raise Brave Kids," *Jen Hatmaker* (blog), January 17, 2013, http://jenhatmaker.com/blog/2013/01/17/brave-moms-raise-brave-kids.

4. Perri Klass, MD, "Are You Overprotecting Your Child?" Parenting.com, 2013, http://www.parenting.com/article/are-you-overprotecting-your-child.

5. Jennifer Gish, "How Not to be a Helicopter Parent," *St. Louis Post-Dispatch*, January 9, 2010, http://www.stltoday.com/lifestyles/how-not-to-be-a-helicopter-parent-real-parenting-sometimes/article_cf860e11-a76f-547c-9b4b-9a73948a2efb.html.

6. Madeline Levine, *The Price of Privilege: How Parental Pressure and Material Advantage Are Creating a Generation of Disconnected and Unhappy Kids* (Harper, 2006).

7. Klass, "Are You Overprotecting Your Child?"

CHAPTER 8—THE HEART MATTERS MOST

1. Danny Silk, *Loving Our Kids on Purpose*.

2. Gary Smalley and John Trent, *The Blessing* (Pocket Books, 1990)

3. Jon Carroll, "Failure is a Good Thing," *This I Believe*, NPR, October 9, 2006, http://www.npr.org/templates/story/story.php?storyId=6196795.

CHAPTER 9—DISCIPLINE

1. Jeff VanVonderen, *Families Where Grace is in Place: Getting Free from the Burden of Pressuring, Controlling, and Manipulating Your Spouse and Children* (Bethany House Publishing, 1992).

2. Silk, *Loving Our Kids on Purpose.*

3. Levine, *The Price of Privilege.*

4. Ibid.

5. Silk.

6. Ibid.

7. "Moms: When No Means No . . . Let's Talk About It," *Tell Me More*, NPR, January 11, 2011, http://www.npr.org/people/5201175/michel-martin.

CHAPTER 10—RESILIENCE

1. Billy Collins, "On Turning Ten," *Billy Collins* (blog), June 24, 2005, http://www.billy-collins.com/page/3/.

2. Philip Yancey, *Disappointment With God* (Zondervan, 1997).

3. Dr. Paul Brand and Philip Yancey, *The Gift of Pain: Why We Hurt and What We Can Do About It* (Zondervan, 1997).

4. Jon Carroll, "Failure is a Good Thing."

5. Dan Miller with Jeanne Zornes, *Living, Laughing, and Loving Life* (Wine Press Pub, 1997).

6. Simon Tugwell, *The Beatitudes: Soundings in Christian Traditions* (Templegate Pub, 1986).

7. Tough, *How Children Succeed.*

CHAPTER 11—SOCIALIZATION

1. Shankar Vedantam, "Social Isolation Growing in U.S., Study Says," *The Washington Post*, June 23, 2006, http://www.washingtonpost.com/wp-dyn/content/article/2006/06/22/

AR2006062201763.html.

2. Robert D. Putnam, *Bowling Alone: The Collapse and Revival of American Community.* (Touchstone Books, 2001).

CHAPTER 12—SOCIAL LIFE

1. Levine, *The Price of Privilege*.

2. Jeff Lawrence, "Finding Companeros," *The Blog of Jeff D. Lawrence* (blog), October 2, 2013, http://jeffdlawrence.com/2012/01/04/finding-companeros-repost/.

3. Saving Jane, "Girl Next Door," *Girl Next Door*, Universal, 2006, compact disc.

4. Rudyard Kipling ,"If," 1895.

CHAPTER 13—CAREER

1. Dr. Temple Grandin and Margaret M. Scariano, *Emergence: Labeled Autistic* (Warner Books, 1996).

CHAPTER 14—EDUCATION

1. John Adams, *Correspondence Between John and Abigail Adams*, Massachusetts Historical Society, http://www.masshist.org/digitaladams/aea/letter/index.html.

2. Levine, *The Price of Privilege*.

3. Ibid

CHAPTER 15—ATHLETICS

1. Levine, *The Price of Privilege*.

2. Stephen Durant, Richard Ginsburg, and Amy Baltzell, *Whose Game Is It, Anyway? A Guide to Helping Your Child Get the Most From Sports* (Mariner Books, 2006).

CHAPTER 16—LOOKING GOOD

1. Sapna Maheshwari, "Victoria's Secret Teen Lingerie Lures Ever-Younger Girls," *Bloomberg*, February 14, 2013, http://www.bloomberg.com/news/2013-02-14/victoria-s-secret-teen-lingerie-lures-ever-younger-girls.html

CHAPTER 17—THE NEW MEDIA

1. "Generation M²: Media in the Lives of 8- to 18-Year-Olds," Henry J. Kaiser Family Foundation, January 20, 2010, http://kff.org/other/event/generation-m2-media-in-the-lives-of/.

2. "AAP Updates Guidance to Help Families Make Positive Media Choices," American Academy of Pediatrics, October 13, 2010, http://www.aap.org/en-us/about-the-aap/aap- press-room/pages/AAP-Updates-Guidance-to-Help-Families-Make-Positive-Media-Choices.aspx.

3. Adam J. Cox, "The Case for Boredom: Stimulation, Civility, and Modern Boyhood," *The New Atlantis*, Spring 2010, http://www.thenewatlantis.com/publications/the-case-for-boredom.

4. Louv, *Last Child in the Woods*.

5. "The Issue," Safety Net: Practicing Innocence Online,

http://safetynet.org.uk/ thefacts.php.

6. Karl Tate, "Internet Pornography Statistics Overview," Top Ten Reviews, http://internet-filter-review.toptenreviews.com/internet-pornography-statistics-overview.html.

7. David Elkind, *The Hurried Child: Growing Up Too Fast, Too Soon* (Perseus Publishing, 2001).

8. Ibid.

CHAPTER 18—MOBILE DEVICES

1. Michael Simon, *The Approximate Parent: Discovering the Strategies that Work with Your Teenager* (Fine Optics Press, 2012).

2. Adam Cohen, "Stuebenville Rape Guilty Verdict: The Case That Social Media Won," *Time*, March 17, 2013, http://ideas.time.com/2013/03/17/steubenville-rape-guilty-   verdict-the-case-that-social-media-won/.

3. Larry Magid, "Family Contract for Online Safety," 2013, http://www.safekids.com/ family-contract-for-online-safety/.

4. Larry Magid, "Child Safety on the Information Highway," 2013, http://www.safekids.com/ child-safety-on-the-information-highway/.

5. "Family Media Agreement: 6–8," Common Sense Media, 2013, http://www.sno.wednet.edu/ files/6013/8014/9769/fma_6_8.pdf .

CHAPTER 19—OUTDOOR LIFE

1. Louv, *Last Child in the Woods*.

2. Ibid.

3. Jake Hindman, personal interview, July 10, 2012.

CHAPTER 20—WORK & MONEY

1. Kay Wills Wyma, *Cleaning House: A Mom's 12-month Experiment to Rid Her Home of Youth Entitlement* (Waterbrook Press, 2012).

2. Brett & Kate McKay, "The Art of Dadliness: How to Get Your Kids to Do Their Chores (And Why It's So Important They Do Them)," September 19, 2012, *Art of Manliness* (blog), http://www.artofmanliness.com/2012/09/19/the-art-of-dadliness-how-to-get-your-kids-to-do-their-chores-and-why-its-so-important-they-do-them/.

3. Mark Gregston, "The Family Citizen," *Parenting Today's Teens* (podcast), May 28, 2010, http://www.heartlightministries.org/blogs/pttradio/2010/05/.

CONCLUSION

1. Andy Gullahorn, "More of a Man," *Reinventing the Wheel*, St. Jerome Music, 2008, compact disc.

RECOMMENDED BOOKS

Chapman, Gary. *The Five Love Languages of Children.*

Elkind, David. *The Hurried Child: Growing Up Too Fast, Too Soon.*

Levine, Madeline. *The Price of Privilege: How Parental Pressure and Material Advantage Are Creating a Generation of Disconnected and Unhappy Kids.*

Louv, Richard. *Last Child in the Woods: Saving Our Children from Nature-Deficit Disorder.*

Oestreicher, Mark. *Understanding Your Young Teen: Practical Wisdom for Parents.*

Silk, Danny. *Loving Our Kids on Purpose: Making a Heart-to-Heart Connection.*

Smalley, Gary, and John Trent. *The Blessing.*

Tough, Paul. *How Children Succeed: Grit, Curiosity, and the Hidden Power of Character.*

Van Vonderen, Jeff. *Families Where Grace is in Place: Building a Home Free of Manipulation, Legalism, and Shame.*

Made in the USA
Lexington, KY
04 January 2014